FROM

PROTOCOL

TEC [illegible]

MOVING FROM FEAR TO FAITH

Godman Akinlabi

TO

FAITH EGBUTU

Enthusia
PUBLISHING

Note: Unless otherwise stated, all Scriptures are from NKJV.

ISBN: 978-978-944-734-3

Published by Enthusia Publishing
3, Remi Olowude Way, Oniru Lekki, Lagos
08170629795
info@enthusia.com

in association with
the Ready Writer literary agency, Lagos
and
Extra Quality Integrated Service Limited

For more information email thereadywriter@ymail.com.

Book Cover design by Debo Adediran

Photo credit to Bunmi Adedipe Photography

Dedication

To all The Elevation Church members. I see greatness in you.

Contents

Introduction

Some people enjoy the feeling of being spooked. They like horror movies, thrillers and images that make them jump, scream and take them by surprise. They find some enjoyment in having their hearts race for those few minutes and the anxiety and perhaps terror of not knowing what's going to happen. There is however one factor that makes this kind of fear enjoyable for the consumers and lucrative for the producers; at the back of their minds, the audience knows that the experience is temporary because it is a work of fiction. There are no zombies seeking to eat them or axe murderers seeking to slay them waiting outside the cinema.

However, if a person is uprooted from the world of make believe to a world where fear and danger is real and the threat of a violent and gory death was truly imminent, there will be very little to enjoy. There aren't many people who can face a real threat of death and still forge ahead. This is why many nations honour their soldiers and veterans. These men and women propelled by a deep sense of loyalty, love and faith in and for their countries, push past the fear of death to fight for a better future. If the heroes of the past did not rise above their fears to fight for freedom and a better future, the world would be a much darker place today.

Everyone at some point in life gets hit with a fistful of fear. A bad medical report, a terrible stock market report, rumours of staff lay-offs, being in a plane when there's bad turbulence, living in a war zone, and many other scenarios. At such times, fear represents more dangerous than a tingling feeling. It suddenly cripples progress, aborts dreams and sabotages destinies. There are also intangible fears that have very tangible repercussions. The fear of rejection can cause a man who should marry a wonderful woman and raise a great family remain single for the rest of his life, the fear of death can cause a person never to enter a plane explore other lands and conquer other territories, the fear of failure can cause a potential world leader to settle for a mediocre risk-free unremarkable life.

The difference between living in victory or in defeat is how you react to the fear. Will you let it intimidate you? Or will you, like a soldier, dare to press forward. When we read through the Bible we see characters like Abraham, Isaac, Jacob, Moses, Joshua, David, Gideon, Elijah, Samuel, Ruth, Esther, Mary, and the Apostles push past their fears to obey God and achieve great things. They founded nations, delivered slaves, fought and won great battles (when the odds were stacked against them) and faced hostile environments. The Bible tells us they achieved these great things by faith. It is reasonable therefore to conclude that faith is more powerful and is superior to fear. How did they become people of such strong faith? How can you? I trust that this book will help you to break free from a life of fear and embrace the victorious lifestyle of faith.

Godman Akinlabi.

Chapter 1

Do Not Fear The Evil Report

2 Timothy 1:5-7: "when I call to remembrance the genuine faith that is in you, which dwelt first in your grandmother Lois and your mother Eunice, and I am persuaded is in you also. Therefore I remind you to stir up the gift of God which is in you through the laying on of my hands. For God has not given us a spirit of fear, but of power and of love and of a sound mind"

When a parent says to a child, 'remember your family name. Remember whose child you are.' That admonition usually stems from pride in some accomplishment or quality that positively distinguishes their family from the others. Such a quality could be academic, vocational, or some character quality like hard work or honesty. This passage of scripture is an excerpt from a letter written by Paul to Timothy, his protégé. Paul was saying, 'Timothy, remember whose child you are. Lois your grandmother was a great woman of faith. So was your mother Eunice. The baton has passed to you Timothy. Don't drop it. They've done their part in showing you the family way, now do your part and take up the challenge.'

What was Timothy going through that prompted Paul to remind him of his identity and lineage of faith? One of the things we can glean from the letters is that Timothy was a young pastor in an impressive church who was having some challenges asserting himself and his authority. For instance in his earlier letter as recorded in 1 Timothy 4:12-14, Paul wrote, 'let no one anyone despise your youth, but be an example to the believers in word, in conduct, in love, in spirit, in faith, in purity. Till I come, give attention to reading, to exhortation, to doctrine. Do not neglect the gift that is in you, which was given to you by prophecy with the laying on of the hands of the eldership.' (Emphasis mine) In both letters Paul saw the need to reiterate the fact that Timothy was called and gifted by God.

Even though you are anointed and equipped for your calling, if you let it, fear or nerves can get the better of you.

Timothy was called to be in the ministry, but he was through tough times that were making him fearful. The fact that you are called or qualified to be where you are does not mean the world will roll over and let you have an easy time. In fact, sometimes, it is when it is well known that you are accomplished that people go out of their way to make life problematic for you just to prove you can fail. Perhaps there were elders in the church that believed that they should have been ordained as pastors. Perhaps some of them had even been at Timothy's naming ceremony! Now 'the little boy of yesterday' was trying to teach them scripture. Some may have told him unequivocally, "You are not suited for this position. You have neither the skill nor experience to succeed. Your presence is an insult and an affront to us all. If you had any sense, you would tender in your resignation before this job gets too hot for you.'

So you might be facing some stiff opposition. You might be the youngest person in your department. You may have to contend with some bullies at school. Your job may require that you learn some skill that you are sure will get the better of you. These are real situations that could scare the average person, but you are not the average person. Hear what the Spirit of the Lord says to you through His Word. 'Remember whose child you are. Remember whose DNA you carry. You are a child of God.'

The words 'do not be afraid' and 'fear not' occur several times in the Bible. What's the big deal in being afraid? Isn't it just a feeling? Isn't it as much a feeling as being happy, sad or excited? Everyone experiences it at some point. Why should being a child of God preclude you from fear? It's important to remember that Adam only felt fear after he sinned in the garden. Genesis 3: 9-10: "Then the Lord God called to Adam and said to him, "Where are you?" So he said, "I heard Your voice in the garden, and I was afraid because I was naked; and I hid myself.""

Sin makes fear a legal alien.

Fear is a manifestation of sin. Up until the time Adam disobeyed God, fear was an alien: An alien personality, an alien feeling, and an alien concept. Prior to his fall, Adam knew exactly who he was. He was created in the image and likeness of God and had the mandate to subdue and dominate the earth. Note the words 'subdue' and 'dominate'. These words infer the need for pressure, exertion, hard work and perseverance. Sometimes we think that God placed Adam in a garden where he would have nothing to do. No, Adam had a huge project. He had to ensure that the whole earth was to his liking and to God's liking. The difference however is that in spite of having a huge responsibility, Adam did not cower and beg God to create other men to help him; he didn't have sleepless nights thinking that he would fail, or spend time wondering whether if he named an animal it would refused to be named but instead attack him… he was confident in who he was. He was made in the image and likeness of God. He had the breath of God in him. If God could do it, he could do it. He was not afraid. Fear was a foreigner Adam had never met… until he sinned.

You can tell when a child knows that he or she has done something wrong. Gone is that happy, carefree demeanour and instead are those nervous, wary, eyes that wonder when you will discover his wrongdoing and punish him for it. It is as if something suddenly takes over the child and makes him anticipate suffering instead of understanding in the hands of his parents or authority figures.

Sin aims to attack your identity and cause you to doubt who you are and who your father is.

Sin gives fear and inroad to visit and torment you. As the fear of punishment may keep a child at arms length from his parents, so also can the fear of punishment keeps us from God and His blessings. However, God has a solution for that too because even after sending Jesus to die on the cross for our sins, He knew that we would have moments of weakness when our old nature would rear its head and we would sin, but He was not willing to have us alienated from Him. God does not want the spirit of fear to be your companion under any circumstance. So He assures us through John his servant in 1 John 1:9: "If we confess our sins, He is faithful and just to forgive us our sins and to cleanse us from all unrighteousness."
The fact that we have victory in Jesus Christ is crucial when dealing with fear. Our understanding and acceptance that the sin issue has already been taken care of is liberating. It will free you from the power of sin and the grip of the spirit called fear.

The Spirit of Fear

'For God has not given us the spirit of fear...'
Fear is not a feeling; it is an entity. It is a spirit that can alter your identity and change the course of your destiny if you choose to host it. Fear actively tries to find a place in your life and once it does, it binds you to itself. The spirit of fear is the spirit of bondage.

Romans 8: 15-16: "For you did not receive the spirit of bondage again to fear, but you received the Spirit of adoption by whom we cry out, "Abba, Father." The Spirit Himself bears witness with our spirit that we are children of God."

God didn't give you fear for a companion. Fear was not selected to walk with you on your journey through life. Rather, God chose, "the spirit of power, and of love and of a sound mind" (2 Timothy 7b). A sound mind is not just about natural intelligence but also about having a spiritual awareness of who you are. This awareness positions you to face any situation from the standpoint of victory. Having a sound mind and good judgement is important you will need to distinguish between the spirit of fear and God's spirit. Fear speaks. In fact fear can be a very powerful orator, painting pictures of great punishment, suffering and abandonment. Fear tries to make you question your salvation. It questions God's love and His availability and postulates that it is more real than God is. Fear says that when it counts the most, God will not be there to help you. These are lies you must discern and cast out from your heart and mind.

God is 'Abba Father'

If at some point in your life somebody you trusted has let you down, you will be tempted to believe that God can let you down too. I remember that I was quite scrawny when I was growing up and as a result, I had to face my share of bullies. This became even more pronounced when I got into boarding school. Boys being boys, attacked smaller kids like me for fun and made our lives miserable. On one occasion, after being beaten thoroughly by one of the bullies, I was in high spirits. You see my elder brother was to visit me that day and I was sure that he would deal with the bully thoroughly. To my shock and utter disappointment, my brother didn't gear up for a fight, but rather said that I needed to rise up to the occasion. So yes, sometimes human beings can let you down- but remember- they are human. I will not let the fact that my brother supposedly abandoned me influence my perception of God. God says He will never leave me nor forsake me. God is a father. My father. And that is a completely different relationship.

A child is usually more confident when he has a parent around. He knows that if push comes to shove, daddy or mommy will stick up for him. When you have a father that cares for you, that loves you, that understands what you are going through, the sense that your father is present makes you want to rise up to the occasion. That confidence might even push a child to act out. It's just that extra thing one has when you know, 'my dad is here. You can't touch me!' That is what the scripture is describing in Romans 8:15 "... we cry Abba father!" No matter what, we can cry out 'daddy!' and God will hear us and come to our aid.

You are born of God.

1 John 5: 4-5: "For whatever is born of God overcomes the world. And this is the victory that has overcome the world—our faith. Who is he who overcomes the world, but he who believes that Jesus is the Son of God?"

This scripture says that overcoming the world is premised on the belief that Jesus Christ is the Son of God. Jesus Christ overcame the world, and in doing so bought as many as will believe in Him the gift of 'sonship'. We became sons by adoption when we received Him as our Lord and Saviour. The foundation of our faith stems from the fact that we have victory in Christ because Jesus dealt with the devil on our behalf. With that understanding, when we hold on to God's Word, we also paint a mental picture of what we are trusting God for coming to pass. You see yourself healed, restored, prosperous, at peace, or whatever you have asked because you believe and you know that God hears and answers your prayers. You are confident that Jesus won the victory for you and that means that you must triumph in every situation. The inexplicable peace of God guards your heart and mind in all situations because you **know** God is working all things together for your good. (Philippians 4:7, Romans 8:28)

However, if this truth is not deeply embedded in your spirit, it is possible for the spirit of fear to squeeze its way in and build a different foundation in your heart. The spirit of fear thrives on a mental picture of negative outcomes. This is why God gave us the spirit of love- to keep our expectations positive. Romans 5:5 (KJV): "and hope maketh not ashamed, because the love of God is shed abroad in our hearts by the Holy Ghost who is given unto us". When you embrace God's love you are not afraid to hope. You are not plagued by fears of failure of disappointment. A hope that finds its root in God's love will not be put to shame.

Two people with the same backgrounds and level of intelligence wait to be called for a job interview. Both profess to be Christians. Yet one is calm and the other is fretful. Different things run through their minds. The calm one is thanking God for His word that says, *"Therefore settle it in your hearts not to meditate beforehand on what you will answer; for I will give you a mouth and wisdom which all your adversaries will not be able to contradict or resist." (Luke 21: 14-15)* while the troubled one is frantically going over possible questions and is coming apart because he is sure he won't have the right answers. He already has a mental picture of the negative outcome of the interview he has not yet attended. The spirit of fear comes from a sense of defeat.

The person who frets and is anxious does not have an understanding of his relationship with God. With God, your life is a series of wins. It is always a win-win with God, even if you don't get the job or you have to go through some tough times, you can go through challenges in peace because you know that at the end you will win. You just know God has something better for you and you look forward to it with positive expectation. *"Nay in all this things we are more than conquerors through him that loves us!" (Romans 8:37 KJV)* That is how the spirit of love, boldness and soundness of mind grows. It stems from an unshakable faith in God.

Chapter 2

Manifestations of Fear

Fear manifests in many different ways- some more harmful than others.

Nervous tension: There is a type of fear or tension that causes adrenalin to pump and propels you to quick thinking and corresponding action. When faced with sudden danger, an important task or a pressure situation, you may experience a rush of energy, which though may feel unpleasant at that moment; galvanises you to action. This is similar to the feeling an athlete might have before a race. The desire and anxiety to do well causes your heart to beat rapidly and your blood to pump faster. It prepares you for action- inactivity is not an option. S ome people, especially procrastinators actually rely on this type of fear to excel. The fear of missing your flight, or not turning in a proposal at work at the due date stirs them to action. This nervous tension that encourages action and creativity is a type of fear but it is not the spirit of fear.

Cautionary Fear: There is a fear that is borne out of knowledge that brings caution and wisdom. For instance not putting your hand in an open flame or on a live wire because you know that you will get burnt or electrocuted. Or not jumping into a pool if you can't swim, because you know that to thrive in deep water, you need to possess a skill that is different from walking. This informed type of fear also differs from the spirit of fear.

Paralysing fear: There is a fear that causes inertia. Now this is the realm where the spirit of fear creeps in. When you are so afraid of failing, that you don't even bother to try. You don't think you can ever get into a university, so you don't take the entrance exams. You believe that certain jobs are for people of a higher class than you are, so you don't send in your application. You don't think that any woman will ever accept you as a husband, so you never get up to ask. This type of fear, though it may not leave you wide-eyed with your heart racing, will leave you living a very mediocre life.

Tormenting fear: 1 John 4:18 says that fear has torment. There is a fear that can be so overwhelming that in induces hysteria. An example is when a person becomes so anxious about a situation that they experience what has been medically called a panic attack. At this point, the spirit of fear is having a field day. If the root of the fear is not discovered and addressed, panic attacks can lead to nervous breakdowns and incapacitate a person. John 10:10: "the thief (devil) has come to steal, to kill and to destroy." (Parenthesis mine) Once the spirit of fear takes root, it can steal your peace as well as your destiny.

Job and his fears.

Job 1: 1-5:

"There was a man in the land of Uz, whose name was Job; and that man was blameless and upright, and one who feared God and shunned evil. And seven sons and three daughters were born to him. Also, his possessions were seven thousand sheep, three thousand camels, five hundred yoke of oxen, five hundred female donkeys, and a very large household, so that this man was the greatest of all the people of the

East.

And his sons would go and feast in their houses, each on his appointed day, and would send and invite their three sisters to eat and drink with them. So it was, when the days of feasting had run their course, that Job would send and sanctify them, and he would rise early in the morning and offer burnt offerings according to the number of them all. For Job said, "It may be that my sons have sinned and cursed God in their hearts." Thus Job did regularly."

Job was a righteous man with a fear problem. He believed in God all right, but He wasn't confident in God's loving kindness. Job made continuous sacrifices to God from the mindset that something may go wrong. He had a negative expectation. There was no foundation of victory in his heart. If Job had been confident about his right standing with God, his sacrifices would have been given from a heart of worship and not as a preventive measure to ward off punishment. The spirit of fear was what fuelled Job's actions. Jobs fears caught up with him. He lost his children, his possessions, his health and all his wealth. He acknowledged his fears when he said, ***"For my sighing comes before I eat, and my groanings pour out like water. For the thing I greatly feared has come upon me,*** *and what I dreaded has happened to me. I am not at ease, nor am I quiet; I have no rest, for trouble comes."* (Job 3: 24–26. Emphasis mine) Fear truly has torment and attracts negative occurrences based on negative expectancy. Always remember; fear attracts the devil while faith attracts God.

Just like faith, fear is a magnet. What you obsess about the most will make its way to you.

You need to be conscious of the spirit of fear's attempts to creep into your life. If you are constantly in a panic about your children, you have become anxious about your career or get jittery about dying because someone you know passed away, that is the spirit of fear trying to worm its way into your heart. Guard against it.

Very early in 2013, I lost two dear friends of mine within a very short period of time. Shortly after that, a member of my congregation told me that his 7-year-old nephew had passed on after a brief illness. Another lady also came weeping profusely, reporting that her cousin was shot and murdered by robbers while he was driving in traffic. At the time, I was holding a prayer summit, and when I heard the news, it was a struggle to attend, much less lead the prayer summit because of the things that were happening around me. I had to get my mind and thoughts under control. The spirit of fear was trying to edge its way into my subconscious. Before long, one could join in the mindset that says that long life is not guaranteed even though God's word says, *'with long life He will satisfy you and show you His salvation.' Psalm 91:16.* You must cast out fear by maintaining your faith in God's word.

Our expectations in life must not be based on other people's experiences. There are some things we may never understand here on earth that will be revealed when we get to heaven. That notwithstanding, the fact still remains that as a Christian you must base your expectations not on what is happening around you but on the word of God which lives and abides forever. Amen!

Common types of fear

The fear of the future: 'Nobody knows tomorrow'. This is a common phrase in everyday usage. Some Christians use it in a pious fashion in an attempt to show humility not realising that it is an incorrect statement. God knows tomorrow and that puts you at an advantage. God is happy to reveal mysteries to those that know Him. You know God and you know that He knows you and loves you. Your conclusion should be that no matter what tomorrow may bring, you are sorted. Jeremiah 29:11-13 *"For I know the thoughts that I think toward you, says the Lord, thoughts of peace and not of evil, to give you a future and a hope. Then you will call upon Me and go and pray to Me, and I will listen to you. And you will seek Me and find Me, when you search for Me with all your heart."* Don't be plagued by the fear of tomorrow. If challenged by this fear, say, 'I may not be able to give the specifics of my future, but one thing is certain. My tomorrows have God in them, and with Him I always have the victory.'

The fear of the unknown: This takes its cue from having a fear of the future. This is when you have some direction about the next step to take, but you are jittery because you do not know the specifics. For instance you may be offered a job in another state, but while you know what state it is and the job description, you cannot predict how your experience will be. Who will you work with? Will they like you? Will you like the environment? Will you excel? Will you die?

Abraham overcame the fear of the unknown. In Genesis 12, God told Abraham (then called Abram) to leave his country and all that was familiar to him and go to a place that God would show him and Abraham obeyed. No wonder he is celebrated as a man of faith. A man with the fear of the unknown or fear of the future will NOT depart. Many people cannot even take a phone call if there is no caller ID! Abraham was confident in his relationship with God and knew that as long as God knew where he (Abraham) was going, he didn't have to stress about the details. It was the spirit of faith, love, power and soundness of mind that governed his actions. Many people seek confirmations before we take risks. We want to be sure the business venture will be lucrative, or that our spouses-to-be are fertile before marriage. There are times when you just have to go on trust and take the plunge. Abraham heard from God. God spoke to him. That was enough for him and it should be enough for you.

The fear of failure: Read this account about Isaac, Abraham's son as recorded in Genesis 26:12-22:

"Then Isaac sowed in that land, and reaped in the same year a hundredfold; and the Lord blessed him. The man began to prosper, and continued prospering until he became very prosperous; for he had possessions of flocks and possessions of herds and a great number of servants. So the Philistines envied him. Now the Philistines had stopped up all the wells which his father's servants had dug in the days of Abraham his father, and they had filled them with earth. And Abimelech said to Isaac, "Go away from us, for you are much mightier than we."

Then Isaac departed from there and pitched his tent in the Valley of Gerar, and dwelt there. And Isaac dug again the wells of water which they had dug in the days of Abraham his father, for the Philistines had stopped them up after the death of Abraham. He called them by the names which his father had called them. Also Isaac's servants dug in the valley, and found a well of running water there. But the herdsmen of Gerar quarreled with Isaac's herdsmen, saying, "The water is ours." So he called the name of the well Esek, because they quarrelled with him. Then they dug another well, and they quarrelled over that one also. So he called its name Sitnah. And he moved from there and dug another well, and they did not quarrel over it. So he called its name Rehoboth, because he said, "For now the Lord has made room for us, and we shall be fruitful in the land."

Sometimes when we hit rough patches, we throw in the towel, thinking that it is better to give up than to be defeated. Isaac overcame the fear of failure when he refused to give up digging wells. It didn't matter if he would have to dig 10 wells; he **knew** he would prosper. He knew that he had the blessing of his father Abraham and that nothing could stop his prosperity. You must learn how to distinguish failure as an event from you being a failure as a person. Isaac knew that he was no failure, and if you understand who you are in Christ, then neither are you. Albert Einstein in his quest to discover the incandescent bulb said after 1,000 failed experiments, 'I have just discovered a thousand ways it should not be done.' Progress! He saw each setback as progress. To him, each experiment was an adventure- an adventure of faith. Faith because he knew at the end something was going to work out and it did. When your foundation is sure, you can be certain the end is of their adventure is victory.

How would you live if you knew it was impossible for you to fail? If perhaps you had some magical genie grant you the gift of super strength? Most likely, if you tried to lift something and it didn't budge the first time, you would confidently try it again- because you believe in that 'special power' that guaranteed you cannot fail. You would not see your attempts as failures but as part of the process. God is so much more than a fictional creature, so don't be afraid or dismayed, just keep digging.

The fear of evil: It is possible to overcome one type of fear but still be tormented by another. For instance Abraham overcame the fear of the future and the unknown but he still had the fear of evil. On two occasions Abraham lied to kings about his relationship with Sarah because he believed that she was so beautiful, the kings would kill him to have her. Abraham feared the evil in men's heart and how that could impact his life. (Read Genesis 12 and 20)

Isn't it strange that someone could be bold enough to leave a life of security, risk death and poverty and travel without knowing his destination on the instruction of an unseen God, yet still be afraid of what a man might do to him *if* in fact any of the kings were attracted to Sarah? The fear of evil still plagued Abraham's mind.

Some people have no fear for their own lives, but fall apart if anything threatens the lives of their spouses or children. Some people can't buy the kind of cars they truly desire because they are afraid they will be robbed on the highway. Others are afraid to take on political assignments because they fear assassination. You can't give the spirit of fear a foothold no matter the circumstance. Your objective should be to be free from any type of fear by developing your faith holistically. There should be no exceptions to your dependence on God. Deal with the fear and banish it from your life.

Now for some people, Job's story offers no comfort because God gave the devil the permission to give Job a hard time. They think, 'what if the devil were to go to God and ask for permission torment me and God says 'yes'?' At the time the devil touched Job, Adam's fall had made him the prince of this world and given the power to torment man. God's boast was that in spite of the devil's advantage, Job would still not bow to him. When Jesus came into the world, He was a man with a difference. Since He had no sin in Him, He operated in a realm of authority that was based on righteousness. Once Jesus defeated the devil, ALL power became His and He bestowed this power on us. Therefore, today, the devil legally has no power to torment you. The Bible says he comes to steal; he is a thief, possessing nothing. He has only wiles, and if you fall for his trickery then you yield your advantage causing him to find a foothold to harm you and whatever is dear to you.

The devil has no authority to touch you. You give him the authority by falling for his wiles, one of which is FEAR.

Gateways to fear

Guard your heart and mind. Some of the programs I watched on television as a kid made me more susceptible to fear as I grew older. I had to renew my mind and reprogram it with God's word and not some figment of someone's imagination. Today, I'm very careful about the kind of cartoons and shows my children watch. Some time ago my younger daughter said to me, 'Daddy, the door of our room keeps opening on its own. It looks like they are some mysterious things in this house.' Initially I was shocked. I couldn't imagine where she got such an idea. Then I asked, 'have you been watching something; you have been watching those television stations I told you not to watch?' She admitted that she had. Programs that harp on ghosts, ghouls, mysteries and magic put ideas into children's heads that can filter into their hearts. Magic must never be more real to your child than the heaven is. I told my daughter that mysterious things could not reside in our house because the Holy Spirit lived with us and that angels were also on guard and watching over us. I also took her to the door and showed her that the wind was causing it to blow open. I spent a lot of time on mental recalibration for her that day because I needed to uproot that spirit of fear that was trying to take hold of her.

As an adult, if you spend all your time watching horror movies, or fetish movies about demonic activity and witchcraft, you open yourself up for the spirit of fear to tell you a thing or two. If you guard your heart from the onset, you will have a lot less work to do later on. Remember that majority of the people in the film industry sell fear, violence or sex. The church sells faith. Nobody else sells faith out there. It may not be popular, but it is precious. Get faith.

Chapter 3

The Faith Perspective.

Two people looking at a 3D object from different angles are likely to have different perspectives if they only stick to what they see in front of them. In fact, if they are really closed-minded, they might assume it is a 2D object with no possible depth or variation to it. Wisdom is having an accurate interpretation of situations. The difference between a wise and a foolish man is not their environment, it is their perception of their environment. They both have different interpretations of the goings-on around them. Your interpretation of your surroundings or your current situation is an offshoot of your perspective. Perspective is dependent on your vision or eyesight. The big question is: What kind of eyesight do you have?

Seeing things from God's Perspective.

One day, a member of our congregation called me to give an update on a medical procedure he went to have done abroad. The doctor's reports while not completely dismal were not particularly encouraging. Just as I was about to launch into a session of encouragement, he said, 'but pastor, you know I am not relying on what the doctors see; I'm relying on what God said. I know I will be healed.' Something leapt in my spirit when I heard that. I answered him with an emphatic 'yes!' That's a person who has good eyesight; that's a person with the God-kind of vision.

To know what kind of vision a person has, listen to the words they speak. *Luke 6: 45: 'out of the abundance of the heart the mouth speaks'.* A doctor once told me that in his experience, most of the people who come out of surgical theatres alive are those who had said they would see their loved ones afterwards. Those who were overly anxious or who said things like, 'I don't know if I am going to make it' were always encouraged to have a positive attitude. He said a person who goes into the theatre frightened had lost the battle even before it started and made the surgeon's job more difficult than it ought to have been. It is far easier to treat a weak body that has a strong spirit than a weak body with an even weaker spirit.

 # Even science acknowledges the effect of fear. Your mental perspective will always influence your physical reality.

Man is a spirit. When we walk in the spirit, we force the natural to conform to our desires. Medical science has seen several people who should be dead simply refuse to die. There are so many testimonies from people who were given three months to live and 30 years later are still going strong. Their spirits took charge of the situation and by seeing things from God's perspective; they forced their bodies to do likewise. Your spirit, though intangible is the most powerful and the most influential part of you. It is who you are. This is why fear attacks your spirit. If it can conquer your spirit, it can conquer you. Unfortunately, man has become so wrapped up by the science and technology, that we have upset the balance of importance and now give more attention to the natural than to the supernatural.

There's a popular book by Robert Schuller titled, *'Tough times never last but tough people do'*. The title is so evocative; it has been the foundation of many sermons and motivational talks. However, sometimes it seems tough times do last. Why are there are people who live as victims all their lives, buckling under one calamity after the other. How come they never got a break from tough times? How come they didn't get seasons of rest and plenty? One thing we must realise however is that tough times are only temporary when **you** are tough. What makes a tough person? It's not physical strength; it is Vision and people of vision do not lie down scared and defeated; they rise up and act. Your interpretation of the tough time will determine if you will stick it out as a 'tough person'. Let's take another look at Paul's letter to Timothy.

"I thank God, whom I serve with a pure conscience, as my forefathers did, as without ceasing I remember you in my prayers night and day, greatly desiring to see you, being mindful of your tears, that I may be filled with joy, when I call to remembrance the genuine faith that is in you, which dwelt first in your grandmother Lois and your mother Eunice, and I am persuaded is in you also. Therefore I remind you to stir up the gift of God which is in you through the laying on of my hands. For God has not given us a spirit of fear, but of power and of love and of a sound mind. Therefore do not be ashamed of the testimony of our Lord, nor of me His prisoner, but share with me in the sufferings for the gospel according to the power of God, who has saved us and called us with a holy calling, not according to our works, but according to His own purpose and grace which was given to us in Christ Jesus before time began, but has now been revealed by the appearing of our Saviour Jesus Christ, who has abolished death and brought life and immortality to light through the gospel, to which I was appointed a preacher, an apostle, and a teacher of the Gentiles. For

this reason I also suffer these things; nevertheless I am not ashamed, for I know whom I have believed and am persuaded that He is able to keep what I have committed to Him until that Day." (2 Timothy 1: 3-12)

Now this is a tough man. In modern language, Paul was saying, 'I'm not bothered by my chains, so you'd better not be. Pity is a useless emotion. I know who I am in Christ. I know why I'm here in prison, and I know how this ends: in victory in Jesus Christ!' He was the one in chains, yet he told Timothy not to be afraid or timid. If you've ever visited a prison, you will know that it is a place that can break down the most ruthless of criminals. Seeing nothing but high insurmountable walls can kill a man's spirit, but Paul was able to see beyond the walls and chains to draw strength and become a 'minister in chains'. This is why the one who ought to have been comforted was doing the comforting. Through the eyes of faith, he could see his destiny fulfilled. Vision makes you tough. Will you look to God that frees or will you look to the chains that bind?

Remember that faith doesn't say there will never be trouble or danger, faith says, 'In spite of all the trouble around me, I will not be afraid. God is with me.' This excerpt from the book of Job typifies what we should remember in times of trouble.

Job 5: 19 -27. He shall deliver you in six troubles, yes, in seven no evil shall touch you. In famine He shall redeem you from death, And in war from the power of the sword. You shall be hidden from the scourge of the tongue, and you shall not be afraid of destruction when it comes. You shall laugh at destruction and famine, and you shall not be afraid of the beasts of the earth. For you shall have a covenant with the stones of the field, and the beasts of the field shall be at peace with you. You shall know that your tent is in peace; you shall visit your dwelling and find nothing amiss. You shall also know that your descendants shall be many, and your offspring like the grass of the earth. You shall come to the grave at a full age, as a sheaf of grain ripens in its season. Behold, this we have searched out; It is true. Hear it, and know for yourself."

Faith vs. Motivation

There is a need to differentiate between faith and motivation. Motivation encourages self-help. It appeals to people's better sides and encourages them to rise to life's challenges. There is nothing wrong with motivation- in fact there is a place for it- but motivational and self-help talks can only be applied in this world; beyond the natural world, they have no impact. Faith is of the spirit. It is rooted in victory that was won for us on Calvary's cross. Faith doesn't say, 'try your best and you will overcome', faith says, 'it is finished. Be still and know that God is God.' Faith is absolute. It makes no contingency plans. It leaves no room for fear.

Faith Foundation

You cannot develop the God-kind of vision if you do not understand the ways of God. You cannot watch gymnasts on television and expect to execute their complex, athletic manoeuvres without studying and engaging in the ways and disciplines of gymnasts. God ways and disciplines are wrapped up in the principle of faith. Faith is often a mystery to man because it is purely spiritual. It is a suspension of everything your physical senses may purport to be true. Faith is God's way; you cannot successfully emulate Him without deciding to become a creature of faith. The good news is that as believers, we have all been dealt a measure of faith (Romans 12:3) so we have the innate potential to see things the way God does. To maximize this potential, you must give yourself to developing your faith through God's word. Romans 10:17: *"So then faith comes by hearing, and hearing by the word of God"*. God's word is the blueprint that breaks down God's nature and character. Studying the word will help you understand God's ways and will increase your faith to the point where you will also begin to see and execute things the way He does.

The first step is to **make God's word the final authority in every situation.** In order to do this, you must have an unwavering and irrational acceptance that God does not and cannot lie. He is who He says He is and He can and will do everything He says. This is the foundation of faith: that we believe that He is, (i.e. that He exists) and that He rewards those who diligently seek him. (Hebrews 11:6) Believing that God is who He says He is means that you have to believe who He says **you** are. It follows that you should boldly say, 'I am who God says I am, I can have what God says I can have, I can do what God says that I can do. Why? Because God said so.'

This foundation will lead you into building a victorious relationship with God as you learn to handle fear, anxiety, agitation or attacks by His word. The word of God gives rest even in the most trying of situations. 1 Peter 5:7: "*casting all your care upon Him, for He cares for you*". When I think of casting my care, I think of throwing it forcefully, or better still, slamming it on God as a wrestler would execute a body slam. Once I deal with that care or fear so roughly, I can walk away knowing that God will never throw it back at me. This is the kind of confidence that liberates us from fear. It is this understanding of God's word that prompted David to say, *'yea though I walk through the valley of the shadow of death, I will fear no evil; for you are with me. Your rod and staff, they comfort me.' (Psalm 23:4)*

So when you hear terrible news: 'the economy is failing, terrorists are attacking, there's a plague killing people…' what will you say? You should speak God's word. Psalm 112:6-7: "*The righteous will be in everlasting remembrance. He will not be afraid of evil tidings; His heart is steadfast, trusting in the LORD.*' Likewise when you are faced with challenges at work, in your family, in your marriage of relationships or in your body, you will say, *1 John 5:4: 'For whatever is born of God overcomes the world. And this is the victory that has overcome the world—our faith.*' We have victory not in our might or in our wisdom or skill, but in Christ. That is our anchor and what overcomes the world- our faith.

Remember that faith to a natural mind is irrational, but it makes all the sense in the world in the supernatural. It is the language and currency of the spirit realm, and what happens there influences what happens in the natural.

Shipwrecked Faith.

We dealt with some types of fear in the previous chapter but I will look at some types of fear that can really shipwreck your faith.

Mark 5: 21-43:
"Now when Jesus had crossed over again by boat to the other side, a great multitude gathered to Him; and He was by the sea. And behold, one of the rulers of the synagogue came, Jairus by name. And when he saw Him, he fell at His feet and begged Him earnestly, saying, "My little daughter lies at the point of death. Come and lay Your hands on her, that she may be healed, and she will live." So Jesus went with him, and a great multitude followed Him and thronged Him.
Now a certain woman had a flow of blood for twelve years, and had suffered many things from many physicians. She had spent all that she had and was no better, but rather grew worse. When she heard about Jesus, she came behind Him in the crowd and touched His garment.

For she said, "If only I may touch His clothes, I shall be made well." Immediately the fountain of her blood was dried up, and she felt in her body that she was healed of the affliction. And Jesus, immediately knowing in Himself that power had gone out of Him, turned around in the crowd and said, "Who touched My clothes?" But His disciples said to Him, "You see the multitude thronging You, and You say, 'Who touched Me?'" And He looked around to see her who had done this thing. But the woman, fearing and trembling, knowing what had happened to her, came and fell down before Him and told Him the whole truth. And He said to her, "Daughter, your faith has made you well. Go in peace, and be healed of your affliction."

While He was still speaking, some came from the ruler of the synagogue's house who said, "Your daughter is dead. Why trouble the Teacher any further?" As soon as Jesus heard the word that was spoken, He said to the ruler of the synagogue, "Do not be afraid; only believe." And He permitted no one to follow Him except Peter, James, and John the brother of James. Then He came to the house of the ruler of the synagogue, and saw a tumult and those who wept and wailed loudly. When He came in, He said to them, "Why make this commotion and weep? The child is not dead, but sleeping." And they ridiculed Him. But when He had put them all outside, He took the father and the mother of the child, and those who were with Him, and entered where the child was lying. Then He took the child by the hand, and said to her, "Talitha, cumi," which is translated, "Little girl, I say to you, arise." Immediately the girl arose and walked, for she was twelve years of age. And they were overcome with great amazement. But He commanded them strictly that no one should know it, and said that something should be given her to eat."

The fear of disappointment: The feeling of being let down or disappointed is a dangerous one because it attacks hope, which in turn attacks faith. 'Now faith is the substance of things hoped for, the evidence of things not seen.' (Hebrews 11: 1) Faith and hope require energy and commitment. When things don't turn out the way you want them to, or you keep putting your energy towards a certain project but experience repeated failure or negative turnouts, you can feel drained and become disheartened and immobilised by this sense of disappointment. Very often Christians who get discouraged eventually adopt a passive stance to that faith project. You might hear them say something like, 'I don't want to raise my hopes again. I will just leave it to God to do whatever He deems fit.' This statement may sound humble and maybe even pious, but it is the exact opposite. This stance is not only defeatist; it denotes anger and unbelief.

Two miracles could have been unrecorded if this woman and Jarius had succumbed to the spirit of fear. Jarius was especially at risk because as soon as he heard his daughter was dead, fear filled his heart. Jesus had to step in immediately and throw a lifeline of faith. He commanded, 'don't be afraid; believe!' Fortunately for Jairus, he latched on to Jesus' words and believed- but many other people would have turned away and given in to grief and disappointment.

The woman who once had an issue of blood had first-hand knowledge of what it meant to be disappointed. She had moved from one physician to the other and never got better, rather she grew worse. Doctors and all sorts of healers had disappointed her for 12 years while she haemorrhaged both blood and money. She was most likely a Jew, so she must have also prayed incessantly to God while giving all sorts of offerings without any reprieve. She was entitled to be a wholesale distributor of the fear of disappointment, but not this woman; tough times had lasted, but she set out to prove that she was even tougher. She had heard about this Jesus who had been going around doing good and healing the sick. She could have deemed him a quack like all the other doctors that she had visited, but no; she dared to hope again. She stirred up her faith and dared to hope for the impossible- 'If I can touch just the hem of his garment, I will be made whole'. I have a feeling that if for some reason this woman wasn't healed that day, she would have done something more drastic. She may have screamed his name, torn his robe or climbed a tree. She was not going to stop trying just because she had been disappointed.

Some ladies trusting God for a future partner throw in the towel far too quickly. They stay in faith for a short while, but at a mere whiff of disappointment, they compromise or lose faith completely. If you want to get married to a godly man then allow your faith to produce him and raise your hopes accordingly. Hope that is based on God's word never ends in shame. What would shameful would be marrying someone who is not God's best for you and meeting the man of your dreams (or hopes) just weeks later. Maybe you thought a certain guy was 'the one' but he ended up breaking your heart. Move on- make sure your faith is still out there, producing your own mate- this guy was simply a distraction. Like Thomas Edison, say, don't say 'I failed in this relationship', just think of what went wrong and say, 'that is one of the things I don't want in a relationship' and channel your faith to produce the right results. Cast out that fear of disappointment, rejection or embarrassment and fortify your faith. Don't waver between letting God sort out your marital destiny and making a plan B for yourself. As Elijah said in 1 Kings 18:21: *"How long will you falter between two opinions?* If the LORD is God, follow Him; but if Baal, follow him."

God's instruction to man in Genesis 1 was clear. Be fruitful. Multiply. Have dominion. Subdue the earth. Sometimes the earth kicks against you and needs to be subdued. If you don't subdue it the first time, keep trying. The mandate has not changed. What you should ask yourself is, 'what am I doing wrong? What can I do differently to get the results I want and God has promised?' There is no place for maintaining the status quo. The devil certainly isn't- he is constantly looking for ways to destroy you. When you fold your hands and say 'whatever will be will be' you abdicate your role as a king and priest and give the devil a free hand to throw whatever he deems fit at you. Passivity is an enemy of faith.

Que sera sera is not faith. Whatever will be will not be. Whatever you exercise your faith to get will be.

I have met several people frozen in a zone of unfruitfulness because they are afraid to try again. They refuse to apply for a new job, start out a new business, to trust God to bless them with a spouse or a child or ask God for healing. They feel that they don't lose anything by staying at status quo. We have often heard, 'nothing ventured, nothing gained.' I'll add to that by saying, **'nothing ventured, nothing gained, and plenty lost.'** The truth is that faith is a spiritual entity that doesn't remain static; it either grows or shrinks in value. If you are not exercising faith, you will grow weaker and be more susceptible to the spirit of fear.

One of the many lessons the Bible teaches to make us balanced, well-rounded believers is perseverance. If we got everything we wanted the first time, we would never know how to endure or be patient or steadfast.

Romans 5; 1-5: "Therefore, having been justified by faith, we have peace with God through our Lord Jesus Christ, through whom also we have access by faith into this grace in which we stand, and rejoice in hope of the glory of God. And not only that, but we also glory in tribulations, knowing that tribulation produces perseverance; and perseverance, character; and character, hope. Now hope does not disappoint, because the love of God has been poured out in our hearts by the Holy Spirit who was given to us."

The fear of disappointment has robbed many people of their destinies because they were too scared to take a chance on God. Perhaps many ladies have refused your marriage proposal. The temporary rejection might hurt but it pales in comparison to the joy that you can experience when you do find your spouse and live many years together. I know people that applied to dozens of companies for jobs and never seemed to get past the preliminary stage. Some gave up while others persevered and kept applying or took steps of faith to start small businesses. Those who persevered and dared to hope for a better future in spite of consistent rejection have a better story today than those that didn't. I know several successful businessmen who have said that they encountered many failures before they attained success. What if they had given up because they were afraid of being disappointed? Thomas Edison is said to have tried to invent the light bulb 10,000 times before he succeeded. 10,000 times. He said he had discovered 10,000 ways not to do it. Perspective. For him, it was a learning process. Have you tried believing God 10 times much less 10,000? In every seeming disappointment, have you learned something new about your walk of faith? Change your perspective, get rid of the fear of disappointment and emerge the conqueror that God created you to be.

The fear of embarrassment: Today, there is so much emphasis placed on not looking like a fool that if one is not careful, you will forfeit faith for this type of fear. Faith is foolishness to man, but the Bible says the foolishness of God is wiser than men and the weakness of God is stronger than men. (1 Corinthians 1:25) Science says that it is foolishness for a 100-year-old man and a 90-year-old woman to mate and have a child. (Genesis 18) Faith says that's wisdom.

The world says it is foolishness to think that a man can walk on water. Faith says it's wonderful not impossible, and then suspends the laws of physics and makes it happen. (Matthew 18) All through the Bible, faith propels God's servants to do seemingly foolish things in public. Elijah risked public ridicule when he soaked his altar with water when he desired God answer with fire. (1 kings 18) The servants at the wedding feast risked embarrassment when they obeyed Jesus and served water to the host in lieu of wine. (John 2) Faith does 'foolish' things. Faith risks ridicule.

The woman with the issue of blood risked ridicule, ostracism and further disappointment when pressed through the crowd and she reached for the hem of his robe. She is a hero of faith, and her story and her endurance was been recorded for us to learn that faith stakes its life on God's word and not man's perception. When Jesus said Jairus' daughter was not dead but asleep, the mourners erupted in laughter and mockery, but Jesus simply turned them out and maintained a faith-filled environment. Psalm 1 says that a blessed man does not sit in the seat of the scornful. Don't keep company with people that will ridicule your faith. I can imagine how the former mourners-turned-mockers felt when they heard the girl was alive. I'm sure they couldn't laugh or poke fun anymore. Faith always has the last laugh.

The fear of rejection: Rejection, like disappointment is something we tend to take very personal. When we feel rejected, we interpret this to mean we are inadequate or not up to standard. When people who are close to us reject us, the tendency is to retreat into a very tiny shell and vow never to expose yourself to a similar occurrence ever again. The fear of rejection cripples one emotionally and can result in a complex, whether inferior or superior. For instance, people who felt rejected by 'popular kids' in their teenage years, grow up discriminatory even in their adult years. They can walk into a new office and decide who the 'popular' people are and dislike them on sight. Their internal strategy is to reject before they are rejected. Employing this defence mechanism only short-changes you because you are immediately closed off to numerous opportunities to relate and connect. The fear of rejection limits your capacity to aspire or dream, which is the exact opposite of what God desires for His children.

Joel 2: 28: "I will pour out my spirit on all flesh and your sons and daughters shall see visions." To see visions means to aspire, it means to dream. The Holy Spirit in us gives us the capacity to dream, to aspire, to be creative and to dare to try out new things. With the fear of rejection, the devil seeks to shut your mind, and stop you from seeing yourself the way God sees you. There are people who were told when they were young that they were too ugly to be actors, so they never pursued that dream. Yet every day they see new artists emerging who are not what the media regards as beautiful. Every day there are new casting calls, but because they fear being rejected, they never even dare to try. You could be a star waiting to happen but because you are crippled by fear, the world will never see you shine.

When it comes to physical appearances, you need to fight that fear of rejection ferociously. I am very burdened when I see relationships where one spouse feels undeserving of the other. A man may feel in awe of his wife because she was the most beautiful, polished woman he every met and he was amazed that she deigned to marry a plain-looking man like him. Or where a wife gains weight after pregnancy and is thrown into insecurity because she thinks her husband finds her unattractive. Husbands you must not criticise your wives post-childbirth. Neither should you compare them with other women or accuse them of not shedding the baby weight quickly. This is cruel and can be damaging to your spouse. You are fearfully and wonderfully made. You are beautiful. It doesn't matter how thin, fat, short or tall you are. It doesn't matter if you are balding or if your hair is bushy and unruly. Accept yourself. Be proud of yourself; even learn to laugh at yourself- not derisively (where you insult yourself so other people won't- another defence mechanism) but with a confident enjoyment of who you are. Until you accept yourself people will not accept you, and anyone who refuses to accept you is clearly undiscerning… he or she simply lacks good taste.

God will never reject you: We all need to feel accepted. God knows that we need to have that comfort of knowing that we belong and are loved and that is why He placed us in families. However families being human, often deviate from His plan of unconditional love, so He made a better plan to adopt us into His own family where rejection is utterly impossible. (Ephesians 1:6) God has adopted us as His own and we can cry out and say 'Abba Father' to Him at any time and be certain that He will not reject us.

The Prodigal Son. Luke 15: 11-24:

"Then he said, "There was once a man who had two sons. The younger said to his father, 'Father, I want right now what's coming to me.' "So the father divided the property between them. It wasn't long before the younger son packed his bags and left for a distant country. There, undisciplined and dissipated, he wasted everything he had. After he had gone through all his money, there was a bad famine all through that country and he began to hurt. He signed on with a citizen there who assigned him to his fields to slop the pigs. He was so hungry he would have eaten the corncobs in the pig slop, but no one would give him any. "That brought him to his senses. He said, 'All those farmhands working for my father sit down to three meals a day, and here I am starving to death. I'm going back to my father. I'll say to him, Father, I've sinned against God, I've sinned before you; I don't deserve to be called your son. Take me on as a hired hand.' He got right up and

went home to his father. "When he was still a long way off, his father saw him. His heart pounding, he ran out, embraced him, and kissed him. The son started his speech: 'Father, I've sinned against God, I've sinned before you; I don't deserve to be called your son ever again.' "But the father wasn't listening. He was calling to the servants, 'Quick. Bring a clean set of clothes and dress him. Put the family ring on his finger and sandals on his feet. Then get a grain-fed heifer and roast it. We're going to feast! We're going to have a wonderful time! My son is here—given up for dead and now alive! Given up for lost and now found!' And they began to have a wonderful time."

Jesus shared the parable of the lost son to emphasize that there's nothing you can do that will make God reject you. Sometimes we are certain God will reject us because of our sins. That's the devil's favourite lie; the truth is that God forgives and forgives absolutely. God is not like man, who expects you to suffer and do penance to get back into His good graces. Don't struggle to be good enough to be above rejection, He won't reject you no matter how you come. One of the things people I counsel struggle with the most is feeling deserving of God's love. They feel burdened by the weight of their sins. You are not a debtor to sin! The price has been paid. Christ has redeemed us from the curse of the law. We are no longer subject to the law of sin and death. Jesus carried our sin and was rejected for our sakes. We do not need to fear rejection any more. Now, if you err, you can say, 'father forgive me and wash me clean' and God will because the price of sin has been paid. Always remember, you are worthy of God's love and forgiveness. You were purchased at a very steep price and are very valuable to God.

Embrace your God-given identity.

The fear of rejection may also lead to developing an approval addiction- the desire to please people around you to the detriment of your needs and God's plans for you. People who fear being rejected often have very low standards because they place great importance on being accepted. Such a person can easily be pressured into alcoholism, drugs, crime and other vices just because they crave a sense of acceptance. Sometimes it isn't even an obvious vice, it is just a pressure to do something you would rather not do simply to curry favour. I know people who studied certain courses just to please their parents, or went to certain schools just to hang on to their old friends. Don't derail your destiny to observe other people fulfil theirs. You are not a nobody. God's plans for you are awesome. He has invested a great deal in you and wants to see you succeed. You need to believe in the potential you have as a child of God. Develop your self-esteem. Self-esteem is derived from your self-identity. That's why you hear people make statements like, 'I don't really know who I am...' Don't derive your identity from your companions or from those whose approval you seek. Who you are is clearly written in God's word. Read it, embrace it and be confident in who God says you are.

A healthy self-esteem drives away fear and intimidation because will not be moved by what others say or think about you. If you have been blessed with a good voice and decide to enter a singing competition but when you get to the venue, the other contestants jeer at you and say they know you can't sing, would you drop out of the competition? Of course not! They don't know you; they don't have an inkling about your capabilities. You should square your shoulders and prepare to show them a thing or two about singing. Finally, on this subject, ensure you place God's word above your feelings. If you feel like a failure, your feelings are contrary to God's word, which says you have the victory in Christ Jesus. So not even your feelings can be trusted. David said, 'why are you downcast oh my soul… put your hope in God'. (Psalm 42:5) He understood that sometimes your emotions run contrary to God's word. You have to rein them in and speak what God's word says. Speak to your soul and say, 'I am moved by the word and not by my feelings. I care more what God says about me than what anyone else says. I care more about pleasing God than pleasing people.' Guard your heart. Nobody, not even your spouse, should be powerful enough to diminish your perception of your value and cause you sorrow. Believe that God loves you and accepts you unconditionally, just like the father of the prodigal son. With that you will go a long way in dealing with feelings of rejection.

The God-kind of faith ACTS.

The proof of faith is positive action. *'Show me your faith without your works,' James said, 'and I will show you my faith by my works.' (James 2: 18)* Genuine faith acts in line with its persuasions- it does not act in isolation. The power of God is movement activated. When I move in the right direction, God causes things to happen.

I remember one occasion when my associate pastor, Tunde and I set out to attend a pastor's conference in California, USA. We agreed that we would do our own driving during this period and it meant that we would need a satellite navigation system (SNS) along with the rental car. Tunde was in the UK at the time and had an SNS, which he could bring on the trip, which was great as it was one less thing to pay for. I met up with him in the UK and from there we flew to the US. We picked up our rental car from the underground lot without a hitch and plugged in the SNS. We waited for the usual welcome tone that would signal the device was waking up but heard absolutely nothing. The device was completely devoid of life. Seeing that neither of us had any clue where we were going, this was far from a welcome development and we tinkered with it incessantly as we willed it to start. Tunde then suggested that we drive out of the lot. I wasn't too keen on the idea because the thought of pulling out into an 8-lane highway without having any direction was not appealing, but I acquiesced and drove out of the lot. The moment we pulled into the street, the SNS sprung to life! We cheered loudly and would have hugged the device if we could; we were that relieved. In a space of one minute we both looked at ourselves and blurted out, 'this is exactly how faith works! Faith without works is dead!' Nothing moves until you move. Now in hindsight, we realised the SNS didn't work because it couldn't acquire a signal underground, but it was still a brilliant faith lesson. We had to overcome our fears, don coats of courage and move. That is the way faith works.

Will you believe God's word? Will you stake your life on it even if it means trying over and over again? Would you speak faith-filled words even if you were publicly ridiculed? Will you believe God even though you have been going through tough times? Faith is a choice. You must decide whom you will give the reins of your life: Faith or fear. I hope you choose faith. I hope a woman who was proclaimed barren decorates her nursery by faith. I hope that a man whose business venture crumbled picks himself up and starts again. I hope that people tormented by sickness will dare to believe that He is the Lord that heals and place a demand on God's power. I pray that you will all have the last laugh, and that it will be a laugh of faith.

Chapter 4

Creating a Fear-Free atmosphere.

1 John 4: 4-5: "For whatever is born of God overcomes the world. And this is the victory that has overcome the world—our faith. Who is he who overcomes the world, but he who believes that Jesus is the Son of God?"

We have victory through our faith that Jesus is the Son of God. Our faith will not overcome the world, out faith has overcome the world. What is left for us to do is enforce our victory. Imagine if as a wrestler you were told to fight in a rigged match. Contractually, everyone, including your opponent, knows that you are the winner of the match. You will walk into that ring with attitude and confidence, knowing that you are simply putting on a show for the crowd. At the end, no matter how ferocious your opponent may appear, you know that you will pin him to the ground while the referee counts to ten. As Christians we are to strut into life with the same confidence knowing that we have a pre-arranged contract that guarantees that in whatever match we fight, we emerge winners. It should be absurd for you to be anxious or

nervous when you go through life's challenges because you should know at the forefront of your mind that you just have to win. The challenge for many believers is that we have forgotten or we do not believe the terms of the contract and go into every battle wondering if we will succeed or if we will get beaten up.
Something tragic happens when you forget that you are a winner. You become unsure of yourself and lose your confidence and your strut. While in the ring, you stagger under every blow, wondering if that will be your last. Very soon, your opponent, will realise that you do not know that you are supposed to win, and will deal more powerful blows in strategic locations. Before you know it, you are on the one pinned to the floor while the referee counts down. Everyone is shocked; coach, fans, manager and your promoter, who orchestrated the deal, is the most shocked of all. It was a done deal, how could you have lost?

If you have a job interview in your father's company, you shouldn't toss and turn through the night from nerves. It's your father's company. You already have the job. You are only attending the interview as a formality- even your interviewer knows that no matter how you do, the job is yours. So you will sleep soundly and only wake up to daydream about your new office furniture. If however, you convince yourself that being a son isn't enough to get you the job and you show up at the interview a nervous wreck, you can actually make what should have been a done deal have a completely different outcome. The interviewer may report to the board that you appear to be unstable and require a few more years to grow before you can take what should be your right.

Fear robs you of your contractual benefits. It makes you forgetful of the fantastic deal you already have and causes you to deal carelessly with your gifts and your callings. Successful athletes will tell you that you have to see yourself as a victor before the race to win. If you see yourself defeated, you probably will be. Victory is the earnest expectation of positive outcome. You must think, speak and expect victory. Fear and an expectation of victory cannot reside in the same space.

A winner who doesn't know he is a winner can't win.

Guard your peace aggressively

I remember a friend of mine who was really having a rough time with his boss. Once he said, 'Pastor it got to a point where I began to hallucinate. I would wake up in the middle of the night and see my boss standing by the door of my room. I would jump up to stand at attention before him before I would realise that I was in my room and no one was there'.

Fear has torment. How could an adult be so frightened of another man? I found out this fear wasn't unique to my friend; everyone in the office was terrified of this man. This friend of mine was so trapped in this environment of fear; he could barely function. Before he could leave for work every day he would psych himself up to face his boss. Finally, he decided to break free and fired his boss by resigning from the job.

It is hard to preserve a victorious expectation when your peace has been eroded. Fear thrives in chaos. Faith thrives in calm. That's why God says, *'be still and know that I am God'. (Psalm 46:10)* Many things will contend for your peace, be they internal, external or both. Bills, the economy, climatic conditions, natural disasters, marital challenges, poor self-esteem or body-image and more will come at you in an effort to make you a victim not a victor. Sometimes you can even care your way into defeat. This is often true about women, whose natural instinct to show love and concern may sometimes result in anxiety and eventually fear. Some mothers fall ill when their children go off to boarding school or leave home for the university. You must be able to distinguish between the responsibility that one should show as a parent, and just plain worry. What happened to your earnest expectation of victory? What are you expecting to happen to your child, good or evil? If good, then act like it. Smile, hug them, speak a blessing over them and expect good news.

You must embrace the peace of God to successfully walk by faith.

Matthew 6: 24-34:
"No one can serve two masters; for either he will hate the one and love the other, or else he will be loyal to the one and despise the other. You cannot serve God and mammon. Therefore I say to you, do not worry about your life, what you will eat or what you will drink; nor about your body, what you will put on. Is not life more than food and the body more than clothing? Look at the birds of the air, for they neither sow nor reap nor gather into barns; yet your heavenly Father feeds them. Are you not of more value than they? Which of you by worrying can add one cubit to his stature? So why do you worry about clothing? Consider the lilies of the field, how they grow: they neither toil nor spin; and yet I say to you that even Solomon in all his glory was not arrayed like one of these. Now if God so clothes the grass of the field, which today is, and tomorrow is thrown into the oven, will He not much more clothe you, O you of little faith? Therefore do not worry, saying, 'What shall we eat?' or 'What shall we drink?' or 'What shall we wear?' For after all these things the Gentiles seek. For your heavenly Father knows that you need all these things. But seek first the kingdom of God and His righteousness, and all these things

shall be added to you. Therefore do not worry about tomorrow, for tomorrow will worry about its own things. Sufficient for the day is its own trouble."

I find it instructive that Jesus first talked about divided loyalties between God and mammon (the god of money) before He went into his teaching about futility of worry. If you think about it critically, the desire for wealth or financial stability is often at the crux of whatever causes anxiety. Even the desire to marry can be traced to a need to dwell in safety and comfort with a spouse and children. People don't marry for sex alone; they want to pull resources together to build a life. So people worry about money- and this leads to divided loyalties. If you worry about money, your faith in God is in question because you have become preoccupied in gaining mammon's favour. You will have to choose. Most Christians will claim to choose God over money, but the proof of your choice is in your decision not to worry.

The world moves at a frantic pace, trying to escape the clutches of poverty but as a child of God that should not be your reality. Still, Jesus knew that worry was not just a habit but also a spirit that was not easily broken. So as He taught the people, He challenged them to have faith in God for little things, knowing that as their faith grew, they would eventually be able to trust Him for big things. It's the same challenge that I throw at you today. Can you trust God to clothe you, feed you or shelter you? Your father knows you need these things and if He can provide them for birds and flowers, why will He not provide them for you? Do you believe His word is true? Can you take Him at His word and bet your life on it?

You can refuse to worry.

Worry is something people often brush aside and even joke about.

Some even say it's just a part of their make-up or it is evidence of their love and care. The truth is that worry rejects God's wisdom, denies His sovereignty and effectively blocks the manifestations of His power. This is because God is moved by faith and worry says loud and clear that you do not have any. Christians tend to rebel against the instruction not to worry especially when faced with dire situations. At such times not worrying is easier said than done. Have you ever had a day that just went wrong from start to finish? Where anxiety and irritations just pile up and end up making a big mess of the entire day? I remember when I almost had one of those days but caught myself just in time.

It was going to be a busy Tuesday. I had to take my daughters to school, hold a staff meeting and a prayer meeting at the office, attend a compulsory function on the other side of town at mid-day, and then go back home to change and prepare for a major event the church was holding in the evening. None of these events were negotiable and I had to achieve them all while juggling the traffic jams Lagos metropolis is known for. So I woke up with all of that on my mind and needing the day to move like clockwork. Just as I was about to drive the kids to school, I noticed that my older daughter was looking unkempt. Her hair, which had been nicely beaded and braided only two days earlier, was a mess with scarcely any beads to speak of. I got really upset with her and scolded her severely and even compared her to her younger sister whose hairdo was still intact. (I felt awful for doing that and later apologised to her because parents should never make comparisons between their children especially when it puts one in a negative light) I drove them to school, still furious and fuming and only came to myself after I had dropped off my now very quiet daughters. I couldn't believe I had just made that entire ruckus because of some missing beads! Not only was I now agitated, my daughter was also subdued because I had ruined her morning. I realised that I woke up tense because I was thinking about all I had to accomplish not what God had to accomplish through me. I decided that I would not do any other thing until I had drenched myself in God's peace. I drove home and meditated on scriptures about peace and God being in charge for about 30 minutes until I literally noticed a change in my heart rate as peace filled me. Then I looked at my day and knew that even if there were any unforeseen developments, God would be there to handle them with me and for me. Interestingly, many things did happen that day that could have caused agitation, but I was very composed. I just listened to God as He gave me the solutions to each challenge. I don't even want to imagine how the day would have gone if I didn't take the time to get rid of anxiety. Thankfully I did and it turned out to be an awesome day.

 # More haste, less speed. Hastening to do things in your own power leads to slow steps taken to fulfilling your destiny.

Some people cannot comprehend a life without worry. One truth that can free you from its clutches is that worry is a useless emotion. It achieves absolutely nothing, but rather often causes poor performance. Worrying when you are caught in traffic doesn't make the traffic disappear. It is more likely to agitate you and cause you to make bad decisions. Worrying about your child's height or weight won't make him any taller or fatter; it just makes you appear irrational and negative. When you are tempted to worry, take action: pray and meditate on His word.
Philippians 4; 6-7: "Be anxious for nothing, but in everything by prayer and supplication, with thanksgiving, let your requests be made known to God; and the peace of God, which surpasses all understanding, will guard your hearts and minds through Christ Jesus."

It is really that simple. Talk to God about the situation. Cast that care upon Him and ask Him to handle it. (1 Peter 5:7) Cast it believing that He will handle it, because He will. Thank Him for hearing and answering you and then rest easy. Be at peace. God is in control. It takes faith to receive and walk in God's peace. Sometimes we reject His peace because we prefer to have it after the manifestation of our petitions and not before. You don't need peace when everything is going well, you need it when it seems all hell has broken lose. Peace is a supernatural gift that comes in the midst of the storm. One way to know if you have truly cast your care upon the Lord and if you are in faith is if you are at peace about that situation. Real faith transcends worry and anxiety and exudes a confident assurance that the power of God is at work on my behalf.

It is also important to meditate on a scripture that addresses your petition. Keep mulling over God's word and His promises to you. Keep it before your eyes and in your heart. Look at it often, mull over it, and speak it to yourself. In doing so you strengthen your faith as the Holy Spirit paints pictures of victory in your heart. God's word strengthens your faith and safeguards your peace. are conscious of it and you can catch yourself when you start to worry.

Show care but refuse to worry.

At some point in your faith walk, you will be asked to show care through worry. In Africa, when you clap your hands and carry your chin dramatically, only then are people sure that you care. Being calm is often equated with callousness or disinterest. However, God's word doesn't change for Africa or any other country with dramatic practices. If He says don't worry, He means just that. Don't ever succumb to the pressure to worry to show that you care. Don't let anyone guilt you out of your walk of faith and if they think poorly of you, always remind yourself that you have to make the choice to please God, not man. Jesus faced such a situation and also had to risk the wrath and disapproval of a friend because He refused to entertain worry.

Luke 10: 38-42

"Now it happened as they went that He entered a certain village; and a certain woman named Martha welcomed Him into her house. And she had a sister called Mary, who also sat at Jesus' feet and heard His word. But Martha was distracted with much serving, and she approached Him and said, "Lord, do You not care that my sister has left me to serve alone? Therefore tell her to help me." And Jesus answered and said to her, "Martha, Martha, you are worried and troubled about many things. But one thing is needed, and Mary has chosen that good part, which will not be taken away from her.""

You can do a good thing in a poor manner. Martha's request wasn't borne out of genuine care and diligence; she was worried about making a good impression and wanted everything to go perfectly. In fact, she accused Jesus of being uncaring because Jesus was ignoring her agitated state. Could He not see she was going through all this trouble for His benefit? Jesus pointed out something very crucial- Martha was getting agitated about the least important thing when the most important thing was going well. Jesus showed up to impart grace and spiritual blessings upon the their family. Seek first the kingdom of God and His righteousness and all other things will be added on to you. (Matthew 6:33) Martha didn't go after the kingdom; she went after human protocol. Jesus did not acquiesce to Martha's request because Mary had displayed an understanding of spiritual things. God was in their midst! It was a time to worship and to listen, food could come later. The Bible does not tell us if Martha sat down and listened to Jesus but I hope she did. Hopefully she did not get offended and miss out on all the blessings God had in store for her.

Don't sweat the small stuff. The things that matter the most should not be at the mercy of the things that matter the least.

Finally, create a fear-free climate by humbling yourself before God. Pride lets in worry and anxiety because pride says, 'I can sort myself out. I can think through this challenge and resolve it with my intelligence.' Therefore humility and submission to God starts with turning the reins over to Him. Don't submit to God by lip service alone. Submit with your actions. Submit by casting your cares upon Him. Submit by receiving His peace.

Chapter 5

The Love, Grace and Favour of God

One major reason why Christians fall from faith to fear is that their faith lacks assurance. *'How do I know that things are going to work out? When will these issues be resolved? I've seen people stand in faith and nothing happened. How do I know that my faith will not fail? How can I be certain that when I believe God I am not gambling?'*

These questions are common ones that Christians deal with in their faith walk. However, while you may seek these assurances as a new believer, it becomes a problem when you are still struggling with the fundamentals of faith years later. It has been established that faith comes by hearing the word of God. To hear God's word and have it mean something to you, you have to believe that God exists and that He rewards those who seek Him whole-heartedly. To take this even further, it is necessary to understand who this God you have come to believe exists is. When you think of the devil, most likely you imagine an evil cunning being that is out for your downfall. What do you imagine when you think of God? It is okay to think of God as powerful, faithful, holy, just and other great adjectives, but if you don't think 'love' first, then you are yet to embrace the essence of who God really is.

We also must understand the unconditional love that God has for us. God is love. It is on this nature that all His other attributes exist. This truth is the major anchor for the faith that we have in Christ Jesus. God loves you with a love that is complete- lacking nothing. There is nothing that you can do to make God love you more or love you less. That is the power of unconditional love. What we have to do is continue in the walk of righteousness, not because God will love us less if we don't but because we find it difficult to believe in unconditional when we sin. When we are not confident in God's love, we lose confidence in his thoughts about us, lose faith in Him, and allow fear into our hearts.

It is because God is love that He is righteous, Holy, Faithful, Powerful, Just and Mighty. Love is the fulcrum on which all other attributes are expressed. Nothing He does is expressed outside love.

Unconditional love is mind-boggling to the average man. Some people have experienced rejection from loved ones whose duty it was to love them like their parents, siblings, spouses, children and other close relatives. Yet God, whom we cannot physically see says, *"if you go through the fire I will be with you, if you go through high waters I will be with you," (Isaiah 43:2)* God says, "My love for you is unconditional and it cannot be compromised. I will always be waiting for you." These are words we long to hear and to believe but how can we when our understanding of the depth of God's love is limited? How can you have complete faith in someone who you are not convinced will never not love you?

To move from fear to faith in a loving God you must accept the following truths:

1. God loves you. He always has and He always will.

2. His love for you did not commence after your salvation. He loved you while you were still a sinner and before you ever came to Christ. (Romans 5: 8) You became aware of His love after you were saved.

3. His love for you cannot be corrupted by you or by anyone else. God cannot change His nature of love even if you want Him to. *2 Timothy 2:13: "Even when we are faithless, He remains faithful. He cannot deny Himself."*

4. His love for you is constant. It neither increases nor decreases. Therefore He doesn't love you 'more' when you are good and 'less' when you are bad.

5. Nothing can separate you from His love. "For I am persuaded that neither death nor life, nor angels nor principalities nor powers, nor things present nor things to come, nor height nor depth, nor any other created thing, shall be able to separate us from the love of God which is in Christ Jesus our Lord." (Romans 8:38-39)

No matter how your natural mind may rebel, God's love for man has always been without question. It has always been man's love for God that has varied. So don't measure God's love by your own attempts at loving Him and your fellow man, believe in the all-encompassing nature of His love and emulate that and not the other way around. Our mistake is that we imagine God to be like our earthly father/mother or authority figure. God was not made in their images, they were made in His, and unfortunately, some of them are poor representations of His nature. So look to the original, look to the word of God for a revelation of God's love and believe and accept it. It doesn't matter if nobody else on earth seems to love you. It doesn't matter if you have been branded a loner, outcast, sinner, black sheep, loser, unattractive, boring, unlovable or any other derisive adjective that anyone can dream up. You need to say this to yourself and believe it.

1. I am 100% loved by God.

2. I don't have to deserve His love. I don't have to earn His love. I already have it; and I will enjoy it.
3. God loves loving me! He doesn't love me out of pity or compulsion. I am precious to Him. He is fiercely protective of me and calls me the apple of His eye. (Zechariah 2:8)
4. God is constantly thinking about me. Good thoughts about me constantly fill His heart and mind. (Jeremiah 29:11)
5. I am secure in God's love. I know that even if the whole world turns against me, I can stake my life on the fact that God won't. God loves me.

Just as your knowledge of the extent of your inheritance determines your spending limit, your awareness of God's unending love for you determines how much you will enjoy Him.

There is no fear in love.

1 John 4:17-19 makes it clear that love and fear cannot co-exist. It is such a powerful scripture; I want you to read it in two translations. The New King James Version (NKJV) and The Message Translation.

"Love has been perfected among us in this: that we may have boldness in the Day of Judgment; because as He is, so are we in this world. There is no fear in love; but perfect love casts out fear, because fear involves torment. But he who fears has not been made perfect in love. We love Him because He first loved us." (NKJV)

"God is love. When we take up permanent residence in a life of love, we live in God and God lives in us. This way, love has the run of the house, becomes at home and mature in us, so that we're free of worry on Judgment Day—our standing in the world is identical with Christ's. There is no room in love for fear. Well-formed love banishes fear. Since fear is crippling, a fearful life—fear of death, fear of judgment—is one not yet fully formed in love.

We, though, are going to love—love and be loved. First we were loved, now we love. He loved us first." (The Message)

The Message Translation says, *"Since fear is crippling, a fearful life—fear of death, fear of judgment—is one not yet fully formed in love."* Perfect love casts out fear- whether the fear of God's judgment or punishment, or the fear of what anything else can do to us. If you grew up with abusive parents or authority figures, whatever love you may have had for them would have been tempered with a fear of punishment. One way you know that you are doing well with your parenting is if your children can still come to you when they have done wrong. They know they will be punished or reprimanded, but the fear of discipline does not colour their overwhelming confidence that you love them wholeheartedly in spite of the wrong they have done or may do in future. If your child should ever truly feel, 'daddy will never forgive me for this' and would rather run away than face you, that child feels more torment in your relationship than love. You have to get back to the drawing board.

Now you may wonder, 'but doesn't the Bible say we should fear God?' Indeed it does.

Luke 12: 4-5: "Dear friends, don't be afraid of those who want to kill your body; they cannot do any more to you after that. But I'll tell you whom to fear. Fear God, who has the power to kill you and then throw you into hell. Yes, he's the one to fear. (NLT)

You know how people say that 'nice guys finish last'? Don't mistake God's loving nature for weakness. Love is not weak. It is the most powerful force that exists. God is love and He is also El-Shaddai. He is almighty, all knowing, a righteous judge, a great conqueror, and is described as a great and terrible God. God is fierce! So never mistake God's mercy and grace for weakness; He is the only one who can punish the spirit, soul and body. The good news though- is that this great and mighty God is on your side. Jesus emphasized that immediately after

He told the people to fear God. Luke 12: 6-7:
"What is the price of five sparrows—two copper coins? Yet God does not forget a single one of them. And the very hairs on your head are all numbered. So don't be afraid; you are more valuable to God than a whole flock of sparrows."

God is on your side; whom shall you fear?

So this great and terrible God who can vanquish any foe with just the breath of His nostrils is in your corner always ready to fight for and defend you- if you can trust Him enough to ask Him to. Believing in God's might, power and love should reflect in the way that you think and act. If the fiercest, most powerful being in the world is willing to lay down His life for you, why would you be scared of little creatures that threaten you? He has never been defeated and

He never will be. So you should rest easy. If you had a ferocious tiger as your household pet, would you be afraid of getting robbed by petty thieves? You would sleep soundly knowing that thieves could only come to your house to die. Be confident in God's love. Your defender is there so you don't be afraid for your life. He will protect you from harm, from accidents, from lack, from danger.

Say this out loud. "I am 100% loved by God. I am perfectly loved by a perfect God. Perfect love casts out fear. Therefore, I am not afraid of failure, I am not afraid of accidents, I am not afraid of lack, I am not afraid of the future, I am not afraid of any man, beast or creature. I am as bold as a lion, and I live victoriously, because as God's child, I have overcome the world.

Handling Doubts

Matthew 4:1-11:
"Then Jesus was led up by the Spirit into the wilderness to be tempted by the devil. And when He had fasted forty days and forty nights, afterward He was hungry. Now when the tempter came to Him, he said, "If You are the Son of God, command that these stones become bread." But He answered and said, "It is written, 'Man shall not live by bread alone, but by every word that proceeds from the mouth of God.'"

Then the devil took Him up into the holy city, set Him on the pinnacle of the temple, and said to Him, "If You are the Son of God, throw Yourself down. For it is written: 'He shall give His angels charge over you,' and, 'In their hands they shall bear you up, Lest you dash your foot against a stone.'" Jesus said to him, "It is written again, 'You shall not tempt the Lord your God.'"

Again, the devil took Him up on an exceedingly high mountain, and showed Him all the kingdoms of the world and their glory. And he said to Him, "All these things I will give You if You will fall down and worship me." Then Jesus said to him, "Away with you, Satan! For it is written, 'you shall worship the Lord your God, and Him only you shall serve.'" Then the devil left Him, and behold, angels came and ministered to Him."

In our journey from fear to faith we will be tempted to doubt God. We will be tempted to believe He is not able, He doesn't care or that He is not there. Doubts rarely come when the going is good. They surface when we are faced with trials and tribulations. When there is hardship, our flesh longs for relief, and the devil will always offer relief that questions God's ability to provide for you. Temptations will always come; even Jesus was tempted, in fact, the Bible says that Jesus was led to the wilderness to be tempted by the devil. This tells me that as you decide to embrace living a life of faith in God, you will be led through some situations that will test your faith. The question is how your faith will hold up when those trying times come? Will it be strengthened or will you let doubts cause your faith to fail?

Jesus modelled how to triumph over doubts and temptations. We have to rely totally on God's word. Sometimes we try to rationalise things in order to take a shortcut forgetting that we are not sufficient in ourselves. You don't have what it takes to handle the devil without God. Victory lies in knowing God's identity, your identity in Him and what God has already said about your situation. Here are four things to remember when doubts come.

1. God is with you. When hard times come, don't automatically assume that God has left you or God is punishing you. You must be confident that all things work for your good because you love God and because you are called according to His

purpose. (Romans 8: 28)

2. You have the upper hand in every situation because God is with you and in you. 1 John 4: 4: "You are of God little children, and have overcome them, because He who is in you is greater than he who is in the world."

3. Temptations don't last forever and you have the inherent ability to triumph over any temptation you are facing. God will never allow you to be tempted more than you can bear and He always makes a way of escape for you when you trust him. (1 Corinthians 10: 13)

4. God has planned a victorious end for you. Your expectation of victory will not be disappointed. (Proverbs 23:18) When we approach God with an expectation we may be afraid that what we are trusting God for may or may not work out but we should never allow our fear to overtake us and lead us into doubt.

You cannot stop temptations from coming but you can stop doubts from growing. Temptations are external; doubts are internal. Choose not to doubt and you will obtain the promise.

The Grace to stand.

Sometimes one may feel backed into a corner when faced with some dire temptations. You know what God's word says you should do, you want to do it, but it seems impossible to muster enough courage or will do it. That's where grace comes in. Grace is supernatural empowerment to do things we would not ordinarily be able to do.
I recall when I was taking my exams for my masters' degree in

International Law and Diplomacy. On this particular day, the paper was a critical one: Jurisprudence and International law. Failing this course meant you failed everything else. With an engineering background, I was certainly feeling the pressure and I remember wishing this 'cup' would pass over me. About 30 minutes to the exam, a classmate of mine walked into the room where we were studying with the question paper for the exam we were about to take. Immediately people huddled around him whispering sighs of relief and even thanks to God for making a way for them! I stood up carried all my items and headed towards the exit. Just as I was about to leave the room, two guys called out to me, but I didn't look back, heart beating, I left the room. I have to tell you; it was God's grace that gave me the strength to put one foot in front of the other. My flesh was being battered from the course. I had already been fighting anxiety all semester and I certainly didn't want to fail. The leaked question paper tempted me like a ray of hope. After all if anyone deserved special help it was me- the science student in the legal world, but I knew that nothing could justify cheating and I received the grace to flee. The interesting thing is that after that situation, three different members of the class came to me for counselling. They didn't know that I was a minister, but they recognised God's nature in me and came to me for help for some very important matters. I hate to think what would have happened to them and to my testimony if I had compromised that day.

Grace is in abundant supply so take advantage of it. We cannot achieve our destinies by our own strength. We can't make heaven by keeping the law. Remember that the law brings sin while grace brings righteousness.

You are Righteous.

Now righteousness means having a right standing with God- a sense that you belong in His presence and that you have a right to speak to Him or make requests. There are places that you cannot have access to without a VIP pass. They are meant for the crème de la crème of society and require a steep price to gain access. Righteousness is like that VIP pass that grants access to God's throne of grace and mercy. It was also bought at a steep price- the blood of Jesus, and as we take hold of the fact that that we have access to God, it creates unshakable faith and boldness to face any challenges life may throw your way.

Righteousness is a gift. Some people feel righteous when they've been good, or they have stayed away from bad habits. Being prim and proper doesn't make you righteous; in fact, the more you try, the more you fall short of God's glorious standard. Man's attempts at righteousness are like filthy rags before the Lord (Isaiah 64:6). There is nothing you can to do with your own strength to get righteous. Only when you become saved by grace, do you become the righteousness of God in Christ Jesus. We are of the circumcision that worship God in the spirit and have no confidence in our flesh. (Philippians 3:3)

Take Your Fears to God.

Hebrews 4: 16:
"Let us therefore boldly to the throne of grace, that we may obtain mercy and find grace to help in time of need."

It may be difficult to boldly ask God for help when you feel condemned by your past sins, but you have to remember what the Bible says about you. You are a new creature in Christ, old things have passed away and everything has become new. (2 Corinthians 5:17) Your past does not determine your current status with God. You need to tell yourself from time to time, 'my faith is not built on experience my faith is built on the word of God'. This is not a license to live sinfully and just say, 'it's in the past', when you are alive to righteousness, you present your body as a holy sacrifice to God. Righteousness creates an awareness of God's will as well as a desire to please God, so by faith, you practise righteousness.

This brings me to two fears that people have about their relationship with God:

1. Fear that they will go back to sin. You have to free yourself from that limiting mindset. 'The path of a good man is like a shining light that shines brighter and brighter unto the perfect day.' (Proverbs 4:18) You are getting better and better each day. You are not the same person that was trapped in a cycle of sin. Stay focused on the light of God's word, which will keep you from stumbling. Also remember that even if you do stumble, that's not the end of it. Get up, repent and keep walking the good walk of faith.

2. Fear that your faith will not be enough. It seemed Peter had a similar condition when Jesus asked him to join him on the water. One minute, Peter was walking on the strength of Jesus command, the next minute; he doubted his faith and began to sink. (Matthew 14) What if you were trusting God for healing and you receive a negative medical report. Do you remain in faith or do you begin to sink? You must always remember that faith in God is the ultimate and since faith is unseen, you do not derive your confidence from things you can see. 2 Corinthians 6:18: 'while we look not at the things which are seen, for the things which are seen are temporal, but the things which are unseen are eternal.' Temporal means, 'subject to change'. The doctor's report can change. Your financial statement can change. Your marital status can change, but God's word will never change.

Grow your measure of faith.

It is important to grow your faith because challenges only get bigger. If you are satisfied with having a tiny measure of faith, when big challenges come, you will crumble under the pressure and succumb to fear. If you can't trust God for your daily bread, how can you trust Him for capital for your new business? You have to deliberately build your faith in God. Start small. You may be broke and not sure how to get your next meal. Look into the word and find the scripture that says God will supply your needs. Meditate on that scripture until it becomes as real to you as your own name and thank God for that meal. God will provide. When He does, let that testimony strengthen your faith and cause you to trust Him for greater things.

You gain victory according to the measure of your faith. You must therefore develop your capacity to believe and trust God by feeding your spirit with God's word and acting in accordance with it. Faith is like a muscle. The first day you go to the gym you may not be able to lift 50kg above your head, but as you stick with it and build muscle mass, you will one day lift 100kg. Build your faith mass to lift heavy spiritual things. The results of growing your faith are as tangible as a bulging muscle- but you must be willing to do the work. Build up yourself in prayer, in the word and in obedience to God.

Create memories that build faith.

Joshua 4: 1-7:
"And it came to pass, when all the people had completely crossed over the Jordan, that the Lord spoke to Joshua, saying: "Take for yourselves twelve men from the people, one man from every tribe, and command them, saying, 'Take for yourselves twelve stones from here, out of the

midst of the Jordan, from the place where the priests' feet stood firm. You shall carry them over with you and leave them in the lodging place where you lodge tonight.'"

Then Joshua called the twelve men whom he had appointed from the children of Israel, one man from every tribe; and Joshua said to them: "Cross over before the ark of the Lord your God into the midst of the Jordan, and each one of you take up a stone on his shoulder, according to the number of the tribes of the children of Israel, that this may be a sign among you when your children ask in time to come, saying, 'What do these stones mean to you?' Then you shall answer them that the waters of the Jordan were cut off before the ark of the covenant of the Lord; when it crossed over the Jordan, the waters of the Jordan were cut off. And these stones shall be for a memorial to the children of Israel forever."

In the Old Testament whenever God did something significant for the people, they built an altar and worshiped God. In the passage above, Joshua had just miraculously led the children of Israel across the Jordan just as Moses had done 40 years earlier when they crossed the Red Sea. The altar was left there to remind them of what God had done for them and to always remember His faithfulness, power and might. God has done marvellous things for you. Learn to build altars that remind you of God's faithfulness. Write them down, talk about them, tell your children, do whatever you have to do to remember. Your memories of God's greatness are valuable arsenal you can use to stomp the devil when he comes with lies. If God has healed you from typhoid fever, if malaria symptoms try to get you down, you can say, 'no way! The God that healed me of typhoid is more than able to keep me malaria-free'. Through that altar you have established strong faith in God in the matters of health and healing.

Memorials are powerful. When David prepared to face Goliath, he said, 'the Lord who delivered me from the paw of the lion and from the paw of the bear, He will deliver me from the hand of this Philistine'. (1 Samuel 17:37) He did not take God's empowerment and enablement fro granted. He made it a memorial in his heart and used it to build himself up when it was time to face another battle.

Take time to build memorials as they help in building your faith. As you record victory in small things, you gain the courage to face bigger things. Faith grows. David had probably chased off wolves that threatened the sheep before he faced a lion. It was from the confidence of slaying the lion that he took on the bear. Don't consider any breakthrough too small and forget none of God's blessings. There are people who have not had a painkiller in decades. They built their faith from when God healed them of a headache, then a bruise, then a stomachache and so on. Today, sickness doesn't stand a chance against them. Build altars and build your faith. Soon you will say, 'the God who delivered me from malaria and typhoid is able to deliver me and my loved ones from cancer.' Amen!

Chapter 6

How to hear from God.

Once I went to minister at a church in Warri, Delta state, Nigeria. The event was slated for a Saturday, so I made flight plans to make it a one-day trip so I could be in our church the following day. I was really conscious of the timing because there was only one afternoon flight out of Warri, which was scheduled for 12.30pm, and I didn't want to miss it. So the plan was to get into the church, share my message without preamble and get out of there in a similar fashion. As soon as my message was over, I looked at my watch and knew I was already cutting it very close and had to leave at once. Suddenly, another minister leaned in close and said, 'relax pastor. My brother works at the airline and he just told me that your flight has been delayed for at least two hours.' With this new reliable information, I relaxed and enjoyed the rest of my visit, knowing that I would still get to the airport in good time, and I did. The Holy Spirit then spoke to me and said I had just enjoyed the benefits of authentic, exclusive information from somebody who was in the know. If I always stayed plugged in to the Holy Spirit, I could always enjoy that privilege. Wouldn't that make life simpler and more productive?

Fear strives in darkness and uncertainty. I remember another occasion when I was to make a trip from the United States to Nigeria; I started chatting with a very nervous man. He had a promotion interview the following day and his flight had been moved four times. He was a wreck and asked me to pray that the current flight would not be cancelled. In my heart I knew the flight would be delayed but not cancelled and told him not to worry, but that was no consolation to him. How did I know it would go? I could only tell him I just knew. We eventually left a few hours later than scheduled but I had been at peace the whole time while he had been troubled. Once again, this experience showed that having inside knowledge brings calm. This time however, while I didn't have the benefit of a staff to brief me, I had God and the information was just as reliable.

We must seek to be informed because ignorance is like walking through a dark pathway; it's unsettling and creates an atmosphere for fear to reign. When a sighted person is suddenly plunged into darkness, he adopts halting steps, will most likely have an increased heart rate and may sustain injury. His eyesight gives him reliable information that inspires his confident gait. That is how life can be to someone who lacks access to divine direction, uncertain, painful and full of fear.

Knowledge banishes fear and brings confidence. When you watch the rerun of a match you already know the outcome, so fretting becomes pointless. However what God promises is far superior to knowing what has happened; He wants you to know what will happen. "For I am God, and there is no other; I am God, and there is none like Me, Declaring the end from the beginning, And from ancient times things that are not yet done, Saying, 'My counsel shall stand, And I will do all My pleasure,' (Isaiah 46: 9b-10) God knows the end from the beginning, and He wants you to know that at the end of the match of your life, you win!

1 Corinthians 2:6 –12:
"Yet when I am among mature believers, I do speak with words of wisdom, but not the kind of wisdom that belongs to this world or to the rulers of this world, who are soon forgotten. No, the wisdom we speak of is the mystery of God—his plan that was previously hidden, even though he made it for our ultimate glory before the world began. But the rulers of this world have not understood it; if they had, they would not have crucified our glorious Lord. That is what the Scriptures mean when they say,

"No eye has seen, no ear has heard, and no mind has imagined
what God has prepared for those who love him."

But it was to us that God revealed these things by his Spirit. For his Spirit searches out everything and shows us God's deep secrets. No one can know a person's thoughts except that person's own spirit, and no one can know God's thoughts except God's own Spirit. And we have received God's Spirit (not the world's spirit), so we can know the wonderful things God has freely given us." (NLT)
Everything shared in the preceding chapters is dependent on having knowledge of God and His word, but it mustn't stop at academic knowledge. As you mature in your walk with God, you should desire to know the deep secrets and mysteries of God. Just as you deepen your relationship with a friend and he or she starts to share intimate details of his or her life, you want God to share secrets with you about things to come. Communication experts always emphasize the need to listen to what a person has to say. You don't want to just hear with your ears alone; you want to listen with your heart so you can discern the full import of the speaker's message. Paul said he felt more comfortable sharing God's wisdom with mature believers, possibly because he felt that would be more receptive to receive God's revealed word. You must yearn to become the sort of person God can share mysteries with. You must build

your faith past rudimentary things and hunger for more of God.

In moving from fear to faith, you must grow beyond handling the fear of death, sickness, rejection, disappointment or whatever the devil tosses at you, and develop the faith to live in the supernatural. Your goal in life is not to overcome the devil; he is already defeated. Your goal is to enforce your victory in Christ and to walk in the fullness of what God has in store for you. The things that God has in store for us are so amazing that the scriptures say, that no eye, ear or mind has been able to grasp it, but if we can look inwards into the realm of the spirit, we will be catapulted to a new dimension of revelation.

Remember the devil is a defeated foe. Don't get so caught up in fighting the devil that you forget to rule and reign.

Hearing from God.

I have had many Christians come to me frustrated because they say they do not hear from God. Everyday, they see or hear about Christians who were led to do something or heard God say they should go somewhere and then great things happen and they wonder what they are doing wrong. Is God selective? Does He choose whom He talks to? No, God speaks to everyone- the truth is, not everyone is disciplined enough to listen. Today Christians wish that God would just speak to them in an audible voice, as they believe He did with the Old Testament saints. God does speak audibly and in spectacular fashions today, but God primarily wants us to relate with Him by faith and not by sight. He doesn't always want to have to send an angel or part the skies. He is right there in your heart, just believe. Remember what Jesus told Thomas when he doubted His resurrection but sought physical proof instead?

Jesus let Thomas see His pierced hands and feet but corrected his attitude. He said, "*Thomas, because you have seen Me, you have believed. Blessed are those who have not seen and yet have believed." John 20: 29*

Also, while God did speak to Old Testament saints in an audible voice some of the time, I don't believe that He always did. I believe that His prophets and servants were so attuned to Him that their spirits heard His spirit. God is a spirit; the primary way of relating with Him is spiritual. The good news is that it isn't far-fetched because we are also spirits, so we have the inherent ability to relate with God on that level. So there's no need to be agitated or nervous about wanting to hear from God, you should desire it because it is your privilege to relate with Him in spirit and in truth. Don't spend all your energy seeking spectacular guidance like the appearance of angels- the visible appearance of angels is solely based on God's sovereignty. God Himself is with us; we have a better promise. Don't chase the spectacular when you already have the supernatural.

Before His ascension, Jesus said He would send us the Holy Spirit, who would show us things to come, teach us all things, and be our helper and comforter. The Holy Spirit in us reveals God's mysteries to us. He is here to guide us in the way to go. We just need to listen to Him. Recognising the voice of the Spirit happens the same way you can recognise the voice of your friend: after familiarity and practice. One usually needs to speak to a person a number of times to be able to pick out that voice in a crowd. There are many voices struggling for your attention- the voice your own imagination, the voices of other people's opinions, the voice of difficult situations, the voice of the tempter and so on. In all of these, how are we to discern the voice of the Hoy Spirit? In 1 Kings 19: 11- 13, Elijah discerned God's voice to be a still small voice.

"Then He said, "Go out, and stand on the mountain before the Lord." And behold, the Lord passed by, and a great and strong wind tore into the mountains and broke the rocks in pieces before the Lord, but the Lord was not in the wind; and after the wind an earthquake, but the Lord was not in the earthquake; and after the earthquake a fire, but the Lord was not in the fire; and after the fire a still small voice. So it was, when Elijah heard it, that he wrapped his face in his mantle and went out and stood in the entrance of the cave. Suddenly a voice came to him, and said, "What are you doing here, Elijah?"

You have to practice being quiet in your spirit to hear God speak to you. This takes practice and there is no better time to start than now. Talk to God and ask Him to help you discern and recognise His voice and leading. Then thank Him and by faith, confess that you know God's voice and start practicing. Now when it comes to the things of God, the Bible is clear that there is a growth pattern from being infant believers to being mature ministers of the gospel. So when you set out to recognise God's voice, start small. Personally, to get myself familiar with God's leading, I started out with little things, like asking God which route to take or asking if a friend I wanted to visit would be home. This may sound mundane, but God leads us even in these little things. I remember hearing of a brother who said that when he was getting dressed he felt uneasy about wearing his red shirt, but wore it anyway, because it looked good on him. When he got outside, some men resembling thugs were chasing a man who was wearing a red shirt, mistook him for the man, grabbed him, and took him to their boss. Fortunately, the boss confirmed that he wasn't their target and he was released. What a different day he would have had if he had simply followed the Holy Spirit's 'mundane' prompting.

Your heart (spirit) houses your spiritual senses. You can see, hear and perceive what God says if you follow your heart.

Start with small things and with time you will start to get familiar with the different ways the Holy Spirit leads you. Don't practice hearing from God when you want to make a major decision- like whom to marry for instance. Start with things that don't have too much at stake. *"Strong meat belongeth to them that are full of age, even those who by reason of use have their senses exercised to discern both good and evil." Hebrews 5: 14 (KJV)* Exercise your senses with smaller things and then move on to more critical things.

For instance, when driving I would ask the Holy Spirit what route was free and then I make a decision based on what I sensed. Sometimes I got it wrong, and get into traffic, but when I got it right, I would register that *feeling* in my heart like an identifier so that the next time I asked the Holy Spirit a question and I had the same feeling, I followed it. People describe the way the Holy Spirit leads them in different ways. Some people liken it to a flash of an idea, a picture or a thought in their minds, others say they feel either uneasy in their hearts or some excitement that prompts them to take action. I know people who have been delivered from accidents because they felt restless and knew that it was the Holy Spirit steering them away from that course of action. It's from practice- first the little things, then the big things.

The Holy Spirit's leading is real. As you stay sensitive to Him, it will seem as real as tangible things. There have been times when I've been so attuned to the His voice that I looked behind me to see if somebody had spoken. It was that real to me and the truth is that it should be that real to all believers. Remember that there's far more to us than what we can perceive with physical senses. The supernatural realm, which we do not see, birthed the physical realm, which we do see. Hebrews 11:2; "By faith we understand that the worlds were framed by the word of God, so that the things which are seen were not made by things which are visible." It makes sense to rely on the source of information for direction.

Seek God's leading on everything. Seek His counsel on the job, when seeking out new clients, working on projects or studying for exams. When I receive invitations to minister at churches or speak at conferences, I ask the Lord if I should go. I live as a man who is under authority. It can be the difference between life and death.

The Word of God

God's word is the foundation of developing an ear to follow Him. God will not instruct you contrary to what He has said in His word. When you interact continually with the word you will be able to discern what God can or cannot say. God will not ask you to cheat on your spouse and steal from your neighbour. I find it difficult to believe that God can speak to a man to divorce his wife in favour of another woman because the Bible says God hates divorce. Yet today people try to sell these things by including a 'God said' to their own lusts and sinful desires. A person who fellowships with the word will not easily have wool pulled over their eyes no matter how spiritual it may sound. I remember the situation of a salesman who paid the proceeds of the sale of his company's products into his account in order to pay the financial vows he made in his church. Apparently he felt that since 'the earth is the Lord's' and he was using it to pay a vow to the Lord, he would be covered spiritually. Nothing was further from the truth and the case was treated like the crime it was. God's word keeps you from error; it doesn't lead you into it.

You have to ensure that His word is deeply buried in your heart. David said, '*Your word I have hidden in my heart so I don't sin against You.*' *(Psalm 119:19)* Remember that the devil tempted Jesus using cleverly twisted scriptures. (See Matthew 4) If Jesus didn't know God's word for Himself, He could have been led astray by the devil. The Bible warns that the devil often appears as an angel of light-donning a cloak of spirituality in order to trip you. It is the word of God that you know that will deliver you from error.

In Psalm 119, David extols God's word, calling it his precepts, ordinances, testament, judgement, commandments and laws. All these words describe something one must live by. David knew that God's word was all He would ever need to get it right in life. As long as He had God's word, He would be all right. I love how he describes God's word in Psalm 119:105: "*Your word is a lamp unto my feet and a light unto my path*" God's word is good for the present and for the future. His word as a lamp to your feet sheds light on your immediate vicinity and as a light to your path, it illuminates the steps in the journey of life.

Develop an appetite for the word.

David clearly had an appetite for the word. Psalm 119 has him declaring that the word is his meat and drink, the word is his treasure, it is all he needs, it is sweeter than honey to him, and it is his life. David's knowledge of God's word fostered their intimate relationship. David knew God's word and God's will. Even when he sinned, he knew how to approach God and ask for forgiveness. David's special relationship was founded on the stability of God's word. David wasn't born with a passion for the word; he developed it. He made the word was his meditation day and night.

Deepening a relationship requires desire. You cannot deepen your relationship with God without desiring what makes Him tick-, which is His word. *1 Peter 2: 2 "as newborn babes, desire the pure milk of the word, that you may grow thereby"*. When you start out in your walk of faith, like a child, you grow on the milk, that is, the simple things and pleasures of God's word. Soon, the child's appetite increases. Your capacity to absorb more from scripture increases. Soon you will desire more than a chapter a day. You will yearn to do character or topical studies... you will ask God about how the prophesies of old will come to pass, you will ask Him to use you like He did the apostles.

Growing your appetite for God's word opens your heart to hear His Spirit. When you read repeatedly that healing is your inheritance, one day, you will feel a prompting in your heart to banish a condition that has plagued you for years. You develop confidence and boldness in God's word. Suddenly, the word no longer reads like a compilation of stories from long ago but an instruction manual for your everyday life. Scriptures that you may have read in the past will become so real to you; you can apply them at work, in your marriage or with your children. When God's word flares up in your heart and gives direction, that is God speaking to you.

Develop a taste for God's word by studying it again and again and again.

Watch your diet

Beware of junk food. Just as stuffing a child with sweets and fast food will derail your goal of a healthy life for your child, engaging in the wrong spiritual diet can keep you from hearing from God. Watch what you read, what you watch or what you listen to. Remember that the goal is to recognise God's voice. It would be very hard to recognise God's voice when you surround yourself with negative influences. Surround yourself with things that will enhance your spiritual growth. Godly books, music, messages and people are instrumental in living a vibrant life of faith.

Get Sensitive

A sinner does not feel remorse for sin because it is his nature. His spirit is dead to God and alive to sin. When you are in Christ your spirit is dead to sin and alive to God. This is why when you sin against God; you know it. You suddenly feel uncomfortable in your own skin. You have acted out of your true character and you sense the need to make it right. It is the devil's nature to be vengeful. A Christian is not comfortable repaying evil with evil. This sensitivity is another way the Holy Spirit gets your attention. Unfortunately, for some people this sensitivity does not last because they do not repent of their actions. With time, their senses become dull to the Spirit's leading.

In the early period of our marriage, whenever my wife and I had a misunderstanding, my first inclination would be to grab my car keys and drive out. Yet each time I looked at the keys, the Holy Spirit would tell me not to go out, but rather to go to another room to cool off. At the time, because my emotions were heightened I would struggle to obey because all my flesh screamed to do was to get out. In fact, it seemed like the wiser thing to do was to leave but because I could discern the voice of the Holy Spirit, I would ask for His help and He always gave me the strength to obey. Developing your sensitivity to God's spirit helps you discern between the voice of God and that of the devil when it counts the most. Now I realise that making a habit of storming out would have driven a wedge between my wife and I or made us believe there was never a way to amicably work out any issues.

When you can discern the voice of the Spirit of God, He can speak to you very specifically especially in times of trouble. There are times when you can sense danger in your spirit, and the purpose of that urgency is not to succumb to fear, but to spend time in intercession. When God leads you to pray for someone's safety or deliverance, you can do so confidently because He reveals to redeem. *James 5: 16: 'the effective fervent prayer of a righteous man avails much'.* He prompts us to pray so that His power is made available to deliver. In Acts of the Apostles 27, Paul, even though a prisoner perceived in his spirit that the ship and its crew were in trouble and told the captain that they would lose their lives if they went on the voyage. He was ignored and soon they were in trouble. While the captain and crew engaged in all sorts of activities to save the boat, Paul prayed and fasted because He knew human efforts would be fruitless and that only God could turn the situation around. Eventually, Paul told them that God had answered his prayer and that even though the boat would be lost, none of them would die, and it happened just as he had said. That's what happens when we are sensitive to God's spirit.

Supernatural peace

Philippians 4: 6-7:

"Be anxious for nothing, but in everything by prayer and supplication, with thanksgiving, let your requests be made known to God; and the peace of God, which surpasses all understanding, will guard your hearts and minds through Christ Jesus."

Another way God speaks or communicates with us is through His peace. Earlier in the chapter I shared my experience on how I knew the flight from the US would not be cancelled. I could not say that God had specifically told me that it wouldn't but I had a peace that it wouldn't, and that was enough for me. It has nothing to do with what is going on around you or what you may be feeling. The peace of God is like a knowing smile that just says everything is going to be okay. It's the sort of peace that says, 'this sickness is not unto death' even though a person is critically ill. It is the peace that says, 'God is Jehovah Jireh. He will provide'. When you have no money in your account to pay the bills. It comes from deep within. It is inexplicable and supernatural and like Paul says, it defies natural human understanding.

When I met my wife, we started out as friends and I had no intention of courting her because I had just come out of another relationship. However, some months down the line, my feelings for her deepened and I felt connected to her. I prayed very intently because I didn't want to make a mistake in choosing a life partner, but God didn't say anything specific, but I had peace. I prayed some more, wanting God to say something or do something but I only got even more attracted to her and still felt nothing but peace. I married my wife on the strength of God's peace and that peace gets stronger every day.
I have learned to believe this scripture and rely on it with all my heart. God's peace is an assurance that He has heard your prayer and He will take care of you. I consider it to be one of the sweetest ways that God speaks to His children.

The Inward Witness
Romans 8:14-16:
"For as many as are led by the Spirit of God, these are sons of God. For you did not receive the spirit of bondage again to fear, but you received the Spirit of adoption by whom we cry out, "Abba, Father." The Spirit Himself bears witness with our spirit that we are children of God,"

Though the Holy Spirit may lead us through feelings of unrest or peace, the Holy Spirit is not a thing or a sensation. He is the Inward

Witness speaking to our spirits causing us to live right. Some people do not feel bold enough to say, 'The Holy Spirit led me to do this, or the Holy Spirit told me to do that'. It is not an unusual thing for God to talk to you; it is normal. It is proof that you are a child of God. It is your right to have conversations with your father and have Him respond to you. Hearing from God is not the exclusive preserve of the clergy; every child of God can hear from Him.

When the Holy Spirit bears witness with our spirits, in other words confirms and gives us that confident assurance that we are indeed children of God, fear flees. Read the same scripture written in the Amplified Version of the Bible:
For all who are led by the Spirit of God are sons of God. For [the Spirit which] you have now received [is] not a spirit of slavery to put you once more in bondage to fear, but you have received the Spirit of adoption [the Spirit producing sonship] in [the bliss of] which we cry, Abba (Father)! Father! The Spirit Himself [thus] testifies together with our own spirit, [assuring us] that we are children of God.

We are free from fear and slavery! When you fellowship with the Lord and let the Holy Spirit speak to you, He will confirm it repeatedly. You are a child of God, you are not a slave to sin, and you have no need to fear.

Conclusion:

- You can live a victorious life that is free from fear and full of faith.

- Remember that God loves you with an everlasting, unconditional love. He will never reject you. You can trust God with everything- body, soul and spirit.

- Remember that faith comes from believing God and taking Him at His word. Your faith will grow as you walk with Him and meditate on His word.

- Remember to cast any fear upon Him and ask Him to strengthen your faith in Him. Faith grows; don't be discouraged.

- Remember your identity. You are who God says you are; nobody knows you like He does.

- Remember your make-up. You are made in the image of God. You do not have the spirit of fear but the spirit of power, love and of a sound mind.

- Remember your ability. You can do what God says you can past disappointments notwithstanding.

- Remember you are not alone. God will never leave or abandon you. He will lead you and guide you.

- Remember to cry out. In times of trouble, He will answer.

- Remember to listen. God always speak to His children. He is speaking to you even now. Open your heart and listen.

- Remember you have won. God has already given you the victory.

Let's make some faith confessions together:

I have victory by the blood of Jesus and by the finished work of Christ on the cross. All things around me are working together for my good. I overcome the spirit of fear because I have victory. Christ did it all; He paid the price for me to come out on top! He paid for me to be bold, confident and to overcome in every situation. I refuse to fear. I will not be dismayed. Greater is He that is in me than He that is in the world. Get out fear! I have no room for you. I only express power, love and soundness of mind. In Jesus name!

If you have found hope and encouragement from reading this book and would like to receive more information about the author, or this ministry, please contact us. God bless you.

The Elevation Church
Telephone: +234 700 ELEVATE (700 353 8283)
E-mail: info@elevationng.org
Website: www.elevationng.org

Follow Godman Akinlabi on these Social Media Platforms:

Twitter:	@pgeeman
Facebook:	Godman Akinlabi